*French Chic*

# FASHION
# KNITTING

**100 IDEES**

BALLANTINE BOOKS · NEW YORK

Conceived, designed and produced by
Conran Octopus Limited
28-32 Shelton Street
London WC2 9PH


*Managing Editor:* Jasmine Taylor
*Contributing Editor:* Philippa Wolledge
*Art Editor:* Caroline Pickles
*Editor:* Diana Mansour
*Illustrators:* Cooper West, Peter Meadows


The editors would like to thank the following for their assistance: Penny Hill, Beryl Miller, *Pingouin* and *3 Suisses* yarns.

Library of Congress Catalog Card Number: 85-91565


ISBN 345-33609-7


Manufactured in Hong Kong


First American Edition: August 1986.


10 9 8 7 6 5 4 3 2 1

**Acknowledgments (Photographer/Stylist)**

1 Olivier Bucourt/A. de Chabaneix-Luntz    4-5 Bernard Maltaverne/Caroline Lebeau
9-11, 13 Patrice Degrandy/A. de Chabaneix-Luntz    16-18 Olivier Bucourt/J. Schoumacher
21-22 Elizabeth Novick/A. Luntz    24-25, 29 Olivier Bucourt/A. de Chabaneix-Luntz
32-7 Yves Duronsoy/J. Schoumacher    38-40 G. de Chabaneix/A. Luntz
44-9 Jerome Tisné/J. Schoumacher    50-51 Elizabeth Novick/A. de Chabaneix-Luntz
55-56 Marcel Duffas/J. Schoumacher    59-62 Olivier Bucourt/A. de Chabaneix-Luntz
64-65 Catherine Caron/A. de Chabaneix-Luntz    67 Gilles de Chabaneix/A. Luntz
69 Clive Streeter    70-73 Daniel Burgi/Garçon
77 Bernard Maltaverne/Caroline Lebeau

# CONTENTS

# INTRODUCTION

The pleasures of knitting make it quite unlike any other craft. What other activity gives you high fashion at half the price of the stores, needs no expensive machinery and can amuse you while you sit in waiting rooms or take long journeys?

But for the real enthusiast, such reasons are only part of the enjoyment. Yarns are such beautiful materials to touch, and the colors available today are more rich, varied and exciting than ever before.

100 IDEES magazine has a unique Gallic flavor, and is renowned for its leading influence in the art of knitting. Its patterns are among the prettiest and most inventive to be found. This collection, from its recent pages, gives a wide variety of projects, for the beginner, the moderately skilled, and a few for those who like to attempt the occasional masterpiece. There are quick cotton tops that would make perfect holiday projects; beautiful chunky cardigans to while away dull winter evenings, and a whole range of exquisitely patterned sweaters that will tempt even the timid knitter to add an exciting new design to their wardrobe.

In every pattern, the original yarn featured in 100 IDEES has been given, but in cases where this may not be readily available a suitable substitute is also included. Colors have been suggested to give you the effect shown in the illustrations. Unfortunately, yarn manufacturers change their ranges every season, to give customers the very latest fashion shades – and sometimes a color may disappear, or even reappear under a different shade name or number. All of these patterns would look just as wonderful in alternative colorways, and will flatter you even more if you choose colors that suit your own skin tones. For example, the Ming Jersey featured first in this book would look just as stunning in black or blue and white.

It is just this versatility that makes knitting so enjoyable, besides the satisfaction that you derive from making something utterly unique.

# BASIC ESSENTIALS

One of the pleasures of knitting is that although the basic skills of casting on and off, knit and purl stitches are simple to learn, they lead on to an almost infinite variety of patterns and textures. It is assumed that people using this book will have mastered the basics and are ready to try more complex types of pattern. If any of the designs include techniques with which you are unfamiliar, the following instructions are intended to show how they should be tackled. They also include details of the finishing touches which make all the difference to the appearance of a knitted garment.

## Abbreviations

The standard abbreviations used in this book are listed below, any further abbreviations are explained within the patterns which contain them.

k = knit
p = purl
st(s) = stitches
st st = stocking stitch
rev st st = reverse stocking stitch
p side = right side
m st = moss stitch
g st = garter stitch
rep = repeat
beg = beginning
patt = pattern
yfd = yarn forward
yrn = yarn around needle
tog = together
SKPO = slip 1, k 1, pass slipped st over
tbl = through back of loop (or loops)
rem = remaining
cont = continue
foll(s) = follow(s)(ing)
alt = alternate
kfb (or pfb) = knit (or purl) into front and back of next stitch
inc = increase
dec = decrease
cm = centimetres

## Tension

The correct tension is given for each pattern. It is easy to rush ahead and start the main pattern without knitting a tension sample first, but a high proportion of failures or at best not-very-successful garments have turned out that way because the knitter did not first make a tension sample.

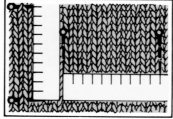

With each design, therefore, we state the correct tension and suggest the number of stitches on which the sample should be worked. Cast on that number and work in the pattern (or stocking stitch if this is the basic stitch used in the design). Knit until the sample measures at least 5in (12cm) and then cast off and measure the tension.

*If the tension is not exactly right, make another sample using larger or smaller needles as necessary to obtain the correct tension.* If you have more stitches to 4in (10cm) than stated, you are working too tightly and should try larger needles; if you have fewer stitches, you are working too loosely and should use smaller needles. Use needles which will produce the correct tension for the main parts of the garment, as given, and remember to make corresponding alterations in the needle size(s) given for any other parts, such as cuffs and waistband.

Although all this can be time-consuming and irritating, especially if you are full of enthusiasm to start on your new project, it is infinitely better than wasting both time and money knitting to the wrong tension.

## Sides

The first row worked is always the right side unless otherwise stated.

'Front of work' refers to the side on which you are actually knitting and 'back' to the side of the work which is away from you: these should not be confused with the terms 'right side' and 'wrong side' of work.

## Swiss darning

Swiss darning is a popular and very simple way of decorating knitted garments by covering the knitting stitch-by-stitch with yarns embroidered on in contrast colors. The effect is almost as if the colors had been knitted in with the garment, but it is generally much quicker and easier to work. Some of the patterns in this book, such as the Wisteria Cardigan (see page 20) already include Swiss darning, but you could also use the technique for some of the other designs, as an alternative to knitting. On the Japanese Wave sweater, for example, on page 39, there are several colors which are only used in very restricted areas, such as the tiny crests of the huge wave. You might find that these are easier to Swiss darn than to knit in with the rest of the pattern.

Swiss darning can be worked either horizontally or vertically, whichever fits in most easily with the motif or pattern. If you are working isolated dots, simply carry the yarn across the back of the work as you would if knitting a Fair Isle pattern. Use a blunt-ended wool needle and, if you are using scrap-bag yarns, make sure that they are thick enough to cover the knitted stitches.

## Horizontal technique

Thread your needle and bring it out at the bottom right-hand corner of the motif, at the base of the first knitted stitch to be covered. Working from right to left, insert the needle behind the stitch immediately above.

Pull the yarn through, then insert the needle back through the base of the first stitch and

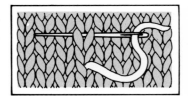

bring it out at the base of the stitch immediately to the left.

Pull the yarn through, covering the first stitch, then work from left to right along the row. When the first row is complete, work back from left to right along the row above.

## Vertical technique

This is worked more like chain-stitch embroidery, which Swiss darning closely resembles. Begin at the bottom, as for the horizontal technique, bringing the yarn through at the base of the first stitch and taking the needle from right to left behind the stitch above. Pull the yarn through and then insert the needle vertically behind the first stitch, as shown. Pull the yarn through to cover the first stitch and continue upwards.

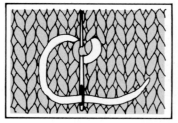

## Jacquard knitting

Many of the designs in this book are examples of the technique known as jacquard. The method of working is quite different from traditional Fair Isle in which two or more colors are carried across the row and used when needed. Jacquard designs either have motifs which may be small or large and are isolated against a background color or else they have large panels or geometric shapes worked in various colors. In all these cases it is necessary to use separate balls of color for each of the different motifs or shapes and if these are large, a separate ball of the background color is also needed for the stitches on each side. Join on the balls where necessary by making a single knot into the previous stitch; afterwards these knots can be unpicked and the ends darned in securely.

To avoid using whole balls of the various colors wind off a small ball for each section; it is more convenient to wind them on to strips of cardboard. Cut a slit in the card so that the yarn can be passed through the slit when it is not being used. It will then hang without becoming entangled. All the spare colors are kept on the wrong side of the work and it is essential each time you begin with a new color to pick it up from underneath the color previously used so that it passes right around the previous color. This will avoid holes forming in the work.

The technique requires practice to avoid the edges of the various sections becoming too loose but once the skill has been mastered spectacular results can be obtained. In many of the designs certain very small sections are embroidered on afterwards by the method known as Swiss darning, which is used to add detail to plain stocking stitch. The stitches are knitted in the background color and are later covered completely with the new color.

## Increases and Decreases

To increase at the beginning of a row either cast on a stitch or work into the front and back of the first stitch. To increase at the end of a

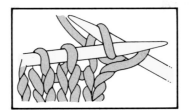

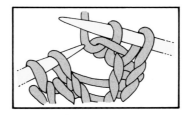

row work into the front and back of the last stitch. In this way it is easier to match the increases at the sides and thus make a neater seam. To decrease at the beginning of a row either cast off a stitch or work SKPO. At the end of a row work the last two stitches together.

## Making up

Once you have knitted all the separate sections of a design, you will be longing to wear the finished article and it is very tempting to rush through the making-up stage. This is a mistake, because a lumpy seam can spoil the effect of hours and hours of careful knitting and if you've waited so long, then it's worth waiting just a little longer to get it right.

## Blocking and pressing

First check the ball band to see whether or not the yarn can be pressed and if so at what heat. If it can be pressed, then each part of the garment must be blocked and pressed before it is seamed.

Blocking is simply a way of putting the pieces under a very

slight tension during pressing. Fold a large towel or blanket to make a thick ironing pad, then lay the piece of knitting right side down on the pad. If there is a measurement diagram, check this as you pin the piece out, pulling it back into shape if it has become distorted. For a back or front, start by pinning at the widest point, which is generally the chest measurement. Push the pins in right up to the head and position them about ½in (1cm) apart all the way around the garment except at ribbed cuffs and hems, which are never pressed.

When the piece is pinned out, cover it with a clean cloth (damp or dry according to the instructions on the ball band): never put the iron directly on the knitting. Press very lightly, lifting the iron up and putting it down on new sections.

## Seaming

Always use a blunt-ended wool needle for seaming. There are several ways of joining a seam. The back-stitch seam is ideal for heavily textured fabrics and for shoulder seams, but the flat seam is also useful for heavily textured knitting, ribbed edges and button bands. The invisible seam is best used for vertical joins only (not shoulders) on straight-sided pieces worked in stocking stitch.

## Method 1 Back-stitch seam

Place the two pieces to be joined with right sides together and begin sewing at the right-hand end of the seam, securing the end of the yarn with two stitches, one on top of the other. Push the needle through both layers and bring it up to the top again. Push the needle in again at the starting point and bring it out a little further

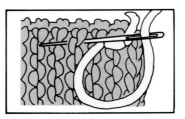

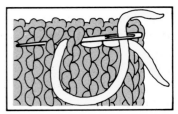

from the point where you last brought it out to make one back-stitch. Continue backstitching to the end of the seam.

## Method 2 Flat seam

Start with right sides together and two stitches, as for the back-stitch seam. Carefully matching rows or stitches, and pushing the needle through vertically for greater accuracy, join the seam with a running stitch effect.

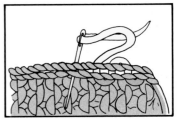

## Method 3 Invisible seaming

Place the two pieces right side up and side by side, matching the rows and edge stitches. Secure the end of the yarn at the bottom right-hand edge and pick up the matching stitch on the left-hand edge. Pull the yarn through tightly, then return to the right-hand edge and pick up the stitch on the next row up. Repeat until the seam is complete.

# MING JERSEY

Oriental artifacts are a perfect source of patterns for handknitting; their symmetry and geometry lend themselves to interpretation in simple stitches. The subtle colors of priceless porcelains can be well matched in the richness of wool, as in this design inspired by a Ming vase. Here, a geometric background is cut through by a band with a leaf pattern.

## CHECKLIST

### Materials

*Bouton d'Or yarns: Superwash (100% laine) 7 (8) balls noir* (**B**); *Cordonnet (acrylique) 5 (6) balls bleu cobalt* (**A**). *Pair each of needles size 1 and 2.*
**Note** *If the above yarn is unobtainable, please refer to page 78.*

### Sizes

*Two sizes, to fit bust 34/36 (36/40) in; 87/92 (97/102) cm. Actual measurements shown on diagram.*

### Stitches used

*Single rib; st st; patt, worked from charts as explained below.*

### Tension

*Over patt using size 2 needles, 28 sts and 32 rows to 4 in (10 cm). Work a sample on 38 sts beg and ending 2 sts from edge of Chart 1.*

## INSTRUCTIONS

### BACK

▦ With size 1 needles and **B** cast on 137 (145) sts and work in rib.
▦ ** *1st row* (right side). P 1, * k 1, p 1; rep from * to end.
▦ *2nd row* K 1, * p 1, k 1; rep from * to end. Rep these 2 rows until work measures 2½ in (6 cm) from beg, ending with a 1st rib row. **
▦ *Inc row* Rib 3 (5), [inc in next st, rib 9 (8)] 13 (15) times, inc in next st, rib 3 (4). 151 (161) sts. Change to size 2 needles and working in st st work patt from Chart 1.
▦ *1st row 1st size* K 3 **B**, * 3 **A**, 4 **B**, 3 **A**, 3 **B**, 3 **A**, 5 **B**, 3 **A**, 3 **B**; * rep from * to * 4 times more, 3 **A**, 4 **B**, 3 **A**, 3 **B**.
▦ *2nd size* K 2 **B**, 3 **A**, 3 **B**, then rep from * to * in 1st size row 5 times, 3 **A**, 4 **B**, 3 **A**, 3 **B**, 3 **A**, 2 **B**.
▦ *Both sizes* Cont in patt as now

set without shaping until work measures 22¼ (23⅜) in, 56 (59) cm from beg, ending with a wrong-side row.
**Neck Shaping** *Next row* Patt 60 (63) and leave these sts of right back on a spare needle, cast off next 31 (35) sts, patt to end. Cont on 60 (63) sts now rem on needle for left back and work 1 row straight.
▦ Cast off at neck edge 5 sts at beg of next row and next alt row and dec 1 st at same edge on foll row. Work 1 row on rem 49 (52) sts then cast off these sts for shoulder.
▦ Rejoin yarns to neck edge of right back sts, cast off 5, patt to end. Cast off 5 sts at neck edge on next alt row, dec 1 st at same edge on foll row then work 2 rows straight. Cast off rem 49 (52) sts.

### FRONT

▦ Work as for back until the inc row at end of welt has been worked. Change to size 2 needles and patt.
▦ *1st row 1st size* K 3 **B**, then rep from * to * in 1st row of back twice, 3 **A**, 4 **B**, 3 **A**, 3 **B**, 3 **A**, 2 **B**, then working from Chart 2 work all the sts shown in 1st row, then k 1 **B**, 3 **A**, 3 **B**, 3 **A**, 5 **B**, 3 **A**, 3 **B**, 3 **A**, 4 **B**, 3 **A**, 3 **B**.
▦ *2nd size* K 2 **B**, 3 **A**, 3 **B**, then rep from * in 1st row of back twice, 3 **A**, 4 **B**, 3 **A**, 3 **B**, 3 **A**, 2 **B**, then working from Chart 2 work all the sts shown in 1st row, then 1 **B**, 3 **A**, 3 **B**, 3 **A**, 5 **B**, 3 **A**, 3 **B**, 3 **A**, 4 **B**, 3 **A**, 3 **B**, 3 **A**, 2 **B**.

▦ *Both sizes* Cont in patt as now set working 75 (80) sts at left side of front and 34 (39) sts at right side from Chart 1 and working the 42 sts of Chart 2 in position established on 1st row. Cont without shaping until 19 rows less have been worked than on back to shoulder edge, thus ending with a p row.
**Neck Shaping** *Next row* Patt 64 (67) and leave these sts of left front on a spare needle, cast off next 23 (27) sts, patt to end. Cont on 64 (67) sts now rem on needle for right front and work 1 row straight.
*** Cast off 4 sts at beg of next row, 2 sts at same edge on next 4 alt rows and 1 st on next 3 alt rows. Cont on rem 49 (52) sts until work matches back to shoulder, ending with same patt row. Cast off these sts. Rejoin yarns to neck edge of left front sts and complete as for right front from *** to end.

### SLEEVES

▦ With size 1 needles and **B**, cast on 61 (65) sts and work as for back welt from ** to **.
▦ *Inc row* Rib 2, [inc in next st, rib 6 (5)] 8 (10) times, inc in next st, rib 2. 70 (76) sts. Change to size 2 needles and working in st st work patt from Chart 1.
▦ *1st row 1st size* K 3 **B**, then rep from * to * in 1st patt row of back twice, 3 **A**, 4 **B**, 3 **A**, 3 **B**.
▦ *2nd size* K 3 **A**, 3 **B**, then rep from * to * in 1st patt row of back twice, 3 **A**, 4 **B**, 3 **A**, 3 **B**, 3 **A**.

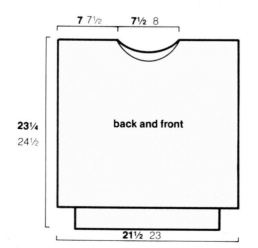

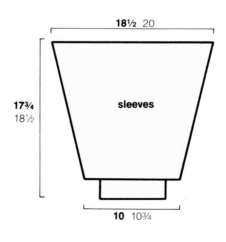

*Blue and black or blue and white are natural combinations for this stunning jersey, but it could work equally well in other porcelain shades. Try fresh green and white for the background, for example, perhaps with splashes of rose pink in the main panel.*

*intricate oriental patterns*

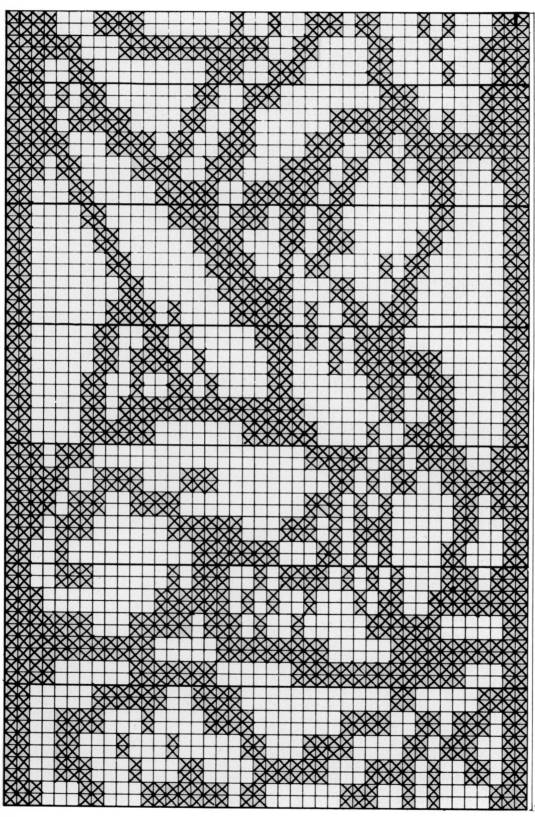

### Chart 2

*Work the complete panel of 42 sts as explained in the instructions for front. This complex chart will be easier to follow if you cross out or cover up each line after you have knitted it.*

66-row patt

1st row

**Chart 1**

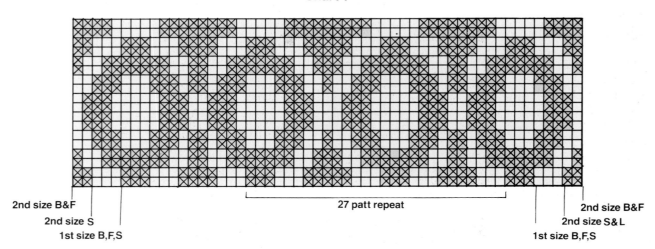

2nd size B&F
2nd size S
1st size B,F,S

27 patt repeat

2nd size B&F
2nd size S&L
1st size B,F,S

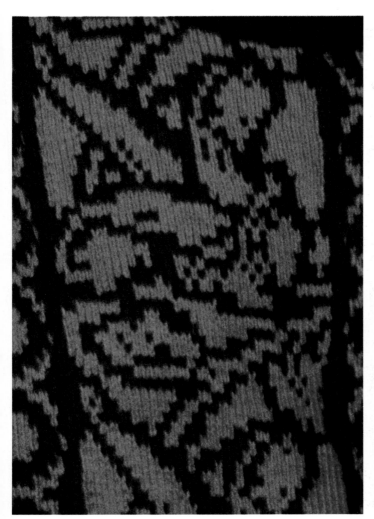

▦ *Both sizes* Cont in patt as now set and work 2 more rows straight then inc 1 st at both ends of next row, then every foll 4th row 27 (28) times, then every alt row 3 times, working extra sts into patt. Cont on 132 (140) sts until work measures 17¾ (18½) in, 45 (47) cm from beg. Cast off all sts.

**NECK BORDER**

▦ With size 1 needles and **B**, cast on 231 (237) sts and work in rib as on back welt for 2¾ in (7 cm). Cast off loosely ribwise.

**MAKING UP**

▦ Join shoulder seams. Join ends of neck border. Placing seam level

with left shoulder seam pin cast-on edge of neck border around neck edges placing it about ⅜ in (1 cm) below neckline. Sew in place as pinned then fold border in half to wrong side enclosing neck edges and slip-st cast-off edge in place. The band is intended to stand away from neckline. Pin cast-off edge of sleeves to sides of sweater placing center of sleeves level with shoulder seams and ensuring that sides of sleeves reach to same position on patt at each side. Sew in place as pinned then join side and sleeve seams.

# WOVEN ROSES

This summery design suggests a sunny trellis covered in climber roses. It is a perfect start to working with two colors as none of the threads are carried very far across the back of the knitting. The roses, too, are easy to work, as they are embroidered in plain panels once the sweater is made.

## CHECKLIST

### Materials
*Berger du Nord yarns in the foll colors:* Qualité Classique: *8 (9) balls beige No 7540* (**A**), *and 5 (6) balls mais* (**B**), *yellow. For the flowers: 1 ball angora 70% in red No 8431 and 1 ball bordeaux No 8430. Pair each of needles size 1 and 2.*
**Note** *If the above yarn is unobtainable, please refer to page 78.*

### Sizes
*Two sizes, to fit bust 32/34 (36/38) in; 82/87 (92/97) cm. Actual measurements shown on diagram.*

### Stitches used
Single rib; st st; patt, *worked from chart, as explained below.*

### Tension
*Over patt using size 2 needles, 28 sts and 32 rows to 4 in (10 cm). Work a sample on 41 sts beg at right-hand edge of chart.*

## INSTRUCTIONS

### BACK
▦ With size 1 needles and **A** cast on 131 (147) sts and work in rib.
▦ ** *1st row* (right side). P 1, * k 1, p 1; rep from * to end.
*2nd row* K 1, * p 1, k 1; rep from * to end. Rep these 2 rows until work measures 2 (2⅜) in, 5 (6) cm from beg, ending with a 1st rib row. **

▦ *Inc row* Rib 7 (8), [inc in next st, rib 12 (9)] 9 (13) times, inc in next st, rib 6 (8). 141 (161) sts. Change to size 2 needles and working in st st work patt from chart.
▦ *1st row 1st size* * K 1 **A**, 9 **B** [1 **A**, 1 **B**] 5 times;* rep from * to * 6 times more, 1 **A**.
▦ *2nd size* K[1 **A**, 1 **B**] 5 times, 1 **A**, 9 **B**; * rep from * to * 7 times

more, 1 **A**.
▦ *Both sizes* Cont as now set and after the 18th row has been worked cont to work the main patt sequence from 19th row to 98th row inclusive, throughout back.
*At same time*, after 60 rows have been worked from chart, work a plain square on which the motif will be embroidered.
▦ *61st row* Patt 70 (80), then k next 31 sts in **A**, join on another ball of **B**, patt rem 40 (50) sts of row. Cont as now set, twisting **B** around **A** at each side of the plain square; work 37 more rows in this way then cut off spare ball of **B** and cont in patt beg with 99th row. Cont until 186 (194) rows have been worked in patt.
**Neck Shaping** *Next row* Patt 55 (63) and leave these sts of right back on a spare needle, cast off next 31 (35) sts, patt to end. Cont on 55 (63) sts now rem on needle for left back; work 1 row straight then cast off at neck edge 5 sts at beg of next row and next alt row. Work 1 row then cast off rem 45 (53) sts for shoulder edge. Rejoin yarns to neck edge of right back sts, cast off 5, patt to end. Cast off 5 sts at neck edge on next alt row, work 2 rows on rem 45 (53) sts then cast off.

### FRONT
▦ Work as for back until 20th row of patt has been worked then work a plain square for motif.
▦ *21st row* Patt 70 (80), then k

next 31 sts in **A**, join on another ball of **B**, patt rem 40 (50) sts. Work 37 more rows as now set then resume patt. Cont until 140th row has been worked then work another square.
▦ *141st row* Patt 10 (20), k next 31 sts in **A**, join on another ball of **B**, patt 100 (110). Cont working this square in same way as before.
*At same time* cont without shaping until 166 (174) rows have been worked in patt.
**Neck Shaping** *Next row* Patt 62 (70) still working the plain square, leave these sts of left front on a spare needle, cast off next 17 (21) sts, patt to end. Cont on 62 (70) sts now rem on needle for right front and work 1 row straight. ***
Cast off 4 sts at beg of next row, 3 sts at same edge on next alt row, 2 sts on next 2 alt rows and 1 st on next 6 alt rows. Cont on rem 45 (53) sts until 192 (200) rows have been worked in patt thus reaching same position as on back shoulder. Cast off.
▦ Rejoin yarns to neck edge of left front sts; cont with the plain square until it is completed then resume normal patt.
*At same time,* complete as for right front from *** to end.

### LEFT SLEEVE
▦ With size 1 needles and **A** cast on 61 (65) sts and work as for back welt from ** to **

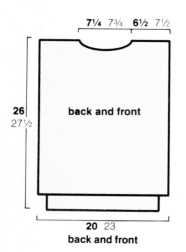

7¼  7¾   6½  7½

26
27½

**back and front**

**20**  23
**back and front**

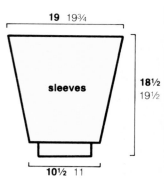

19   19¾

**sleeves**

18½
19½

10½  11

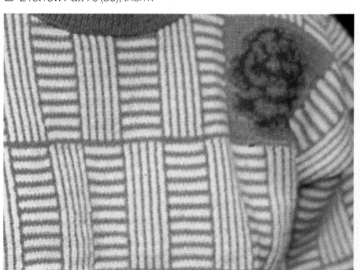

*rambler roses on a trellis*

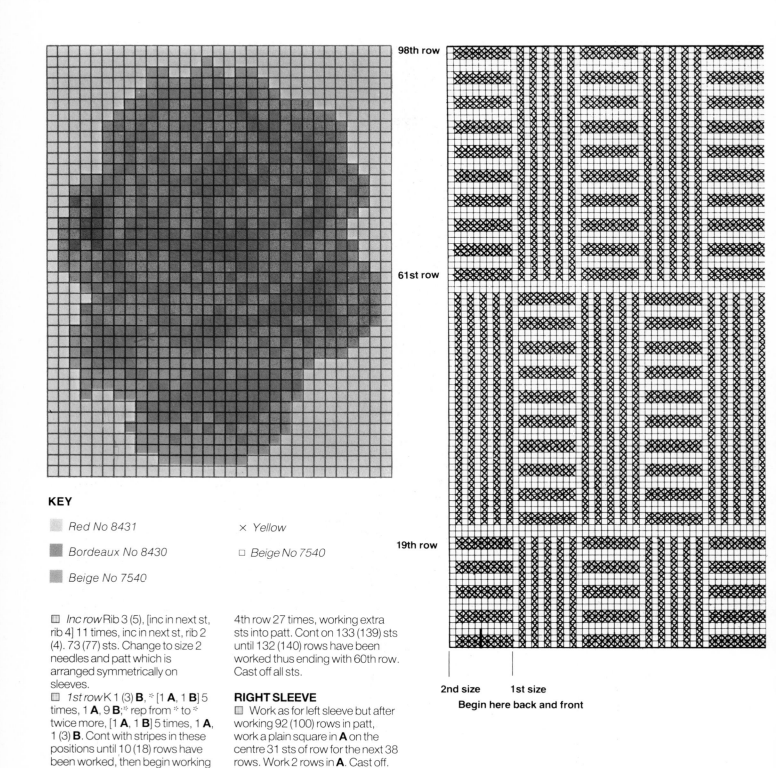

**98th row**

**61st row**

**19th row**

## KEY

Red No 8431

Bordeaux No 8430

Beige No 7540

× Yellow

□ Beige No 7540

**2nd size**    **1st size**

**Begin here back and front**

▦ *Inc row* Rib 3 (5), [inc in next st, rib 4] 11 times, inc in next st, rib 2 (4). 73 (77) sts. Change to size 2 needles and patt which is arranged symmetrically on sleeves.

▦ *1st row* K 1 (3) **B**, ⁎ [1 **A**, 1 **B**] 5 times, 1 **A**, 9 **B**;⁎ rep from ⁎ to ⁎ twice more, [1 **A**, 1 **B**] 5 times, 1 **A**, 1 (3) **B**. Cont with stripes in these positions until 10 (18) rows have been worked, then begin working the patt sequence from 19th row to 98th row inclusive.

*At same time*, after 5 rows have been worked in patt inc 1 st at both ends of next row, then every foll 6th row 2 (3) times, then every foll

4th row 27 times, working extra sts into patt. Cont on 133 (139) sts until 132 (140) rows have been worked thus ending with 60th row. Cast off all sts.

## RIGHT SLEEVE

▦ Work as for left sleeve but after working 92 (100) rows in patt, work a plain square in **A** on the centre 31 sts of row for the next 38 rows. Work 2 rows in **A**. Cast off.

## NECK BORDER

▦ With size 1 needles and **A** cast on 141 (147) sts and work in rib as on back welt for 2 in (5 cm). Cast off loosely ribwise.

14

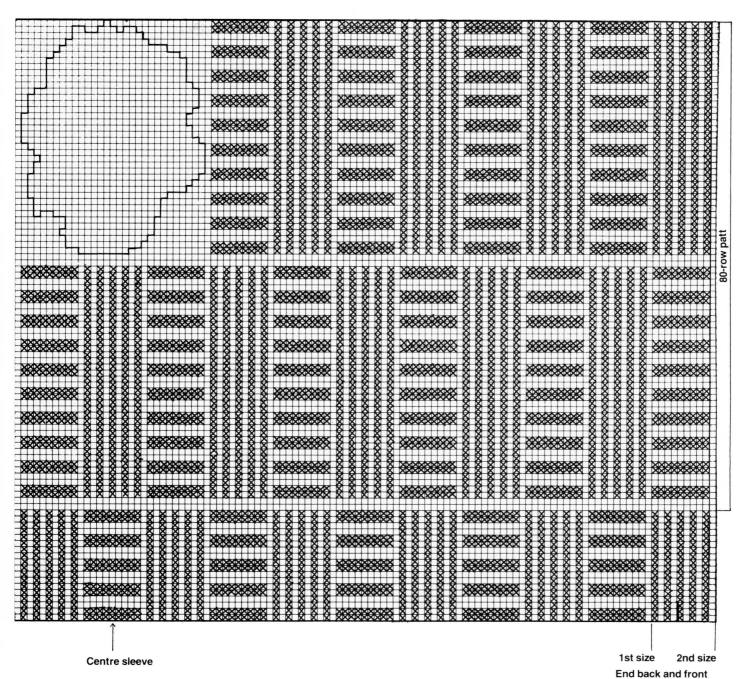

80-row patt

**Centre sleeve**

1st size    2nd size
**End back and front**

**MAKING UP**

Embroider the rose motif in the plain squares using the Swiss Darning method described on page 6. Join shoulder seams. Join ends of neck border. Placing seam at left shoulder pin cast-on edge of border around neck edges placing it a little below the neck edges. Sew in place then fold border in half to wrong side and slip-st cast-off edge in place, enclosing neck edges. Pin cast-off edge of sleeves to sides of sweater placing center of sleeve level with shoulder seam and ensuring that sides of sleeves reach to same position on patt at each side. Sew in place as pinned then join side and sleeve seams. On side seams take care to match patt changes so that patt appears continuous.

*Work the stripes on back, front and sleeves as indicated on the chart. The rose motifs are embroidered on the large plain squares. The position for the back square is shown on the chart; see instructions for the correct placing of the two squares on the front and the one on the right sleeve.*

# SILKEN SHIMMER

The 'crackle glaze' effect on this superb silk sweater is an evocative reminder of warmth in faraway places and makes a luxurious summer cover-up. Bands of black and blue are chic, and they help you to achieve half the design before the patterning begins!

## CHECKLIST

### Materials
*Anny Blatt Silk Anny: 13 balls blue/black No 1731 (A), 3 balls light blue No 1729 (B), and 2 balls gray No 1967 (C). Pair each of needles size 5 and 7.*

### Sizes
*Two sizes, to fit bust 32/34 (36/38) in; 82/87 (92/97) cm. Actual measurements shown on diagram.*

### Stitches used
*Single rib; st st; patt, worked from charts as explained below. When working the patt cut off short lengths of **C** yarn using a separate length for each line so that the yarns are not carried across more than 2 or 3 sts; for larger motifs wind off a small ball of **C**. Always twist **C** around **A** when beg each line or motif in **C**.*

### Tension
*Over st st using size 7 needles, 18 sts and 24 rows to 4 in (10 cm). Work a sample on 24 sts.*

## INSTRUCTIONS

### BACK

▦ With size 5 needles and **A** cast on 85 (91) sts and work in rib.

▦ *1st row* (right side). P 1, * k 1, p 1; rep from * to end.

▦ *2nd row* K 1, * p 1, k 1; rep from * to end. Rep these 2 rows until work measures 2 in (5 cm) from beg, ending with a 1st rib row.

▦ *Inc row* Rib 6 (9), [inc in next st, rib 11] 6 times, inc in next st, rib 6 (9). 92 (98) sts. Change to size 7 needles and beg with a k row work in st st. Work 2 (6) rows **A**, then [12 rows **B**, 12 rows **A**] twice, 12 rows **B**. ⁑ Now begin motifs from Chart 1, on left back, joining on 2 short lengths of **C** as explained above.

▦ *1st row* K 44 (50) **A**, then working from chart k 24 **A**, 5 **C**, 12 **A**, 1 **C**, 6 **A**. Cont working from chart as now set, without shaping until 52nd row has been worked.

**Neck Shaping** *53rd row* K 36 (38) **A** and leave these sts of right back on a spare needle, then with **A** cast off next 20 (22) sts, then patt to end. Cont on 36 (38) sts now rem on needle for left back keeping patt correct; work 1 row

straight. Cast off at neck edge 6 sts on next row and 2 sts on next 2 alt rows. Work 60th row of chart to complete patt. Using **A**, k 1 row on rem 26 (28) sts then cast off for shoulder edge. Rejoin **A** to neck edge of right back sts, cast off 6, p to end. Cast off 2 sts at neck edge on next 2 alt rows, then work 3 rows on rem 26 (28) sts. Cast off.

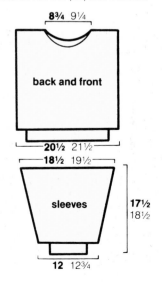

8¾  9¼

**back and front**

20½  21½

18½  19½

**sleeves**

17½
18½

12  12¾

*pure silk for a summer sweater*

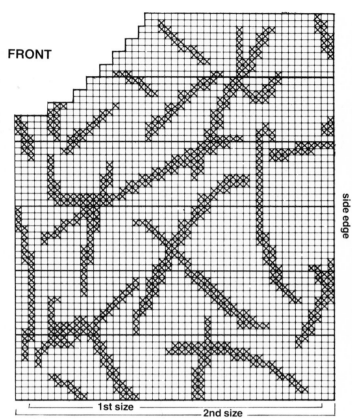

**FRONT**

## FRONT

▦ Work as for back to ✷✷ then begin motifs from Chart 2 on left front.

▦ *1st row* Working from chart, k 20 **A**, 2 **C**, 8 **A**, 3 **C**, 5 **A**, 2 **C**, 9 **A**, then k rem 43 (49) sts in **A**. Cont working from chart as now set, without shaping until 46th row of chart has been worked.

▦ **Neck Shaping** *47th row* Patt 39 (41) and leave these sts of left front on a spare needle, cast off next 14 (16) sts, then using **A**, k to end. Cont on 39 (41) sts now rem on needle for right front using **A** only; work 1 row straight. ✷✷✷ Cast off 4 sts at beg of next row, 3 sts at same edge on next alt row, 2 sts on next 2 alt rows and 1 st on next 2 alt rows. ✷✷✷ Work 2 rows on rem 26 (28) sts then cast off for shoulder edge.

▦ Rejoin yarn to neck edge of left front sts and keeping patt correct cont as for right front from ✷✷✷ to ✷✷✷. Cont on rem 26 (28) sts and work 2 rows to complete the chart then k 1 row in **A**. Cast off.

## LEFT SLEEVE

▦ With size 5 needles and **A** cast on 47 (51) sts and work in rib as on back welt for 2 in (5 cm), ending with a 1st rib row.

▦ *Inc row* Rib 5 (7), [inc in next st, rib 5] 6 times, inc in next st, rib 5 (7). 54 (58) sts. Change to size 7 needles and beg with a k row work 4 (6) rows in st st then begin patt from Chart 3.

▦ *1st row* K 8 (10) **A**, 2 **C**, 4 **A**, 2 **C**, 2 **A**, 2 **C**, 1 **A**, 2 **C**, 3 **A**, 3 **C**, 18 **A**, 1 **C**, 6 (8) **A**. Cont from chart as now set but inc 1 st at both ends of 5th, 11th, 15th, 21st rows and so on at intervals of 4 rows and 6 rows alternately as shown on chart. When the last incs have been worked on 75th row of chart cont on 84 (88) sts until the 88th row of chart has been worked. Work 2 (4) rows in **A** then cast off all sts.

## RIGHT SLEEVE

▦ Work as for left sleeve but working entirely in **A**.

## NECK BORDER

▦ Join right shoulder seam. With right side of work facing and using size 5 needles and A, pick up and k 55 (57) sts round front neck edge and 46 (48) sts across back neck. Beg with 2nd row work in rib as on welt for 5 rows then cast off loosely ribwise.

## MAKING UP

▦ At this stage it is advisable to darn in all the ends of yarn used for the motifs to prevent the yarn slipping through. Join left shoulder seam and ends of neck border. On each side edge mark a point 9 (9½) in, 23 (24) cm down from shoulder seam for armholes and sew cast-off edge of sleeves between marked points. Join side and sleeve seams matching stripes at sides.

side edge

1st size    2nd size

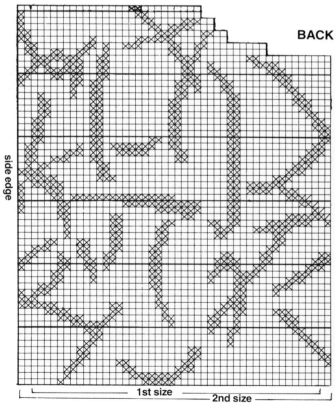

**BACK**

side edge

1st size    2nd size

**SLEEVE**

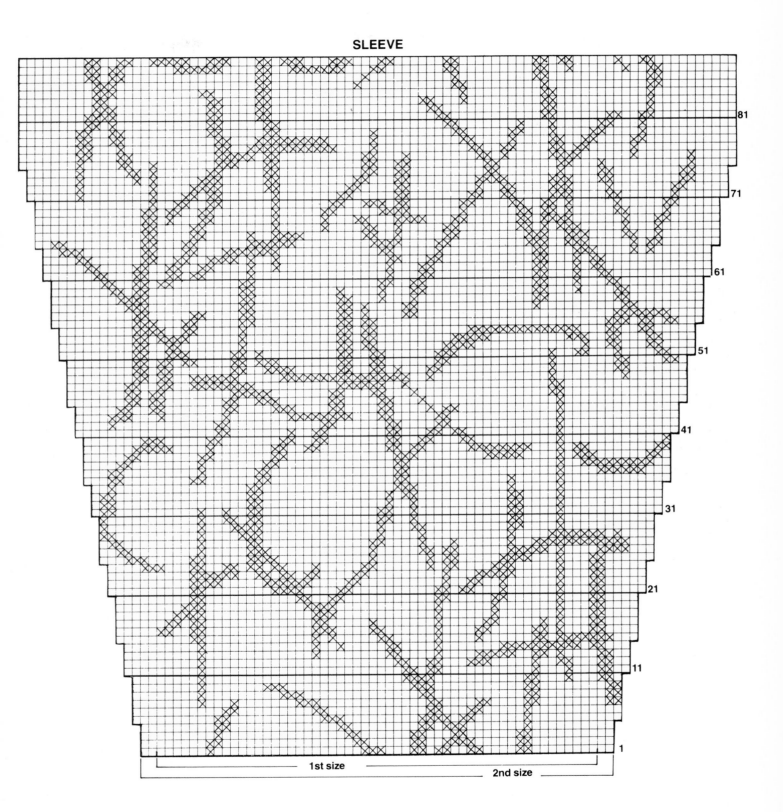

81

71

61

51

41

31

21

11

1

1st size

2nd size

# *WISTERIA CARDIGAN*

This floral cardigan with a 1940s, romantic look has a tie-neck, and set-in sleeves emphasized with padded shoulders for a flattering, contemporary line. The trails of wisteria are knitted in, using simple stocking stitch, but the leaves are embroidered on afterwards to enrich the surface. The front borders and the ties are knitted in a moss stitch to give a raised effect.

## CHECKLIST

**Materials**
*Georges Picaud* Georges Swing: *10 (11) balls No 1 (gray); quality* Orient Express, *3 balls No 8 (mauve); quality* Feu Vert, *1 ball No 66 (green). Pair each of needles size 1, 2 and 3; 4 buttons; pair of shoulder pads.*
**Note** *If the above yarn is unobtainable, refer to page 78.*

**Sizes**
*Two sizes, to fit bust 32/34 (36/38) in, 82/87 (92/97) cm. Actual measurements shown on diagram in centimetres.*

**Stitches used**
Single rib; st st; m st. *For the motifs work from charts as explained below. Wind off a small ball of* **B** *for each flower motif.*

**Tension**
*Over st st using size 3 needles, 24 sts and 32 rows to 4 in (10cm). Work a sample on 30 sts.*

## INSTRUCTIONS

### BACK

▦ With size 1 needles and **A** cast on 111 (119) sts and work in rib.
▦ ** *1st row* (right side). P 1, * k 1, p 1; rep from * to end.
▦ *2nd row* K 1, * p 1, k 1; rep from * to end. Rep these 2 rows until work measures 1¼ in (3 cm) from beg, ending with a 2nd rib row and inc 1 st in centre of last row. ** 112 (120) sts. Change to size 3 needles and working in st st begin motifs from charts.
▦ *1st row* K 0 (2) **A**, now working from Chart No 1, k 31 **A**, join on a ball of **B** and k 1 **B**, then k 23 **A** to complete chart; k the center 2 (6) sts, then working from Chart No 2, k 23 **A**, join on another ball of **B**, k 1 **B**, then k 31 **A** to complete the chart, k 0 (2) **A**. Cont in patt as now set working only the flower motifs; the leaves are embroidered later. *At same time*, when 10 rows have been worked in st st inc 1 st at both ends of next row, then every foll 10th row 7 times more, keeping these extra sts at sides in **A**; after incs are completed there are 8 (10) sts in **A** outside the charts. Cont on 128 (136) sts until work measures 13 (13⅜) in, 33 (34) cm, from beg, ending with a p row.
▦ **Armhole Shaping** Cast off 4 sts at beg of next 2 rows, 2 sts at beg of next 8 rows and 1 st at beg of next 4 (6) rows. 100 (106) sts. Now inc 1 st at both ends of every foll 6th row 6 times then cont on 112 (118) sts until work measures 20½ (21¼) in, 52 (54) cm from beg, ending with a p row. For 1st size a few rows rem to be worked from charts; (for 2nd size charts should be completed).
▦ **Shoulder and Neck Shaping** *1st row* Cast off 9, k until there are 36 (38) sts on right needle, leave these for right back, cast off next 22 (24) sts, k to end. Cont on 45 (47) sts now rem at end of needle for left back and cast off 9 sts at beg of next row. *** Cast off 3 sts at neck edge on next row and 9 sts at shoulder edge on foll row; rep last 2 rows once. Cast off 3 sts at neck edge on foll row then cast off rem 9 (11) sts to complete shoulder slope. Rejoin yarn to neck edge of right back sts and complete as for left back from *** to end.

### LEFT FRONT

▦ With size 1 needles and **A** cast on 55 (59) sts and work as for back welt from ** to **. 56 (60) sts. Change to size 3 needles and working in st st work patt from Chart No 1.
▦ *1st row* K 0 (2) **A**, then working from chart k 31 **A**, join on **B** and k 1 **B**, then k 23 **A** to complete chart, k 1 (3) **A**. Cont in patt as now set and work 9 more rows without shaping. For side shaping inc 1 st at beg of next row then at same edge on every foll 10th row 7 times more keeping these extra sts at side in **A**. Cont on 64 (68) sts until work matches back to armhole, ending at side edge.
▦ **Armhole Shaping** Cast off 4 sts at beg of next row, 2 sts at same edge on next 4 alt rows and 1 st on next 2 (3) alt rows. 50 (53) sts. Now inc 1 st at same edge on

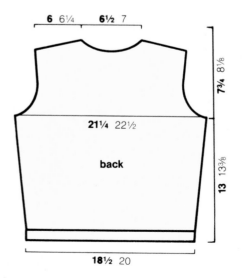

6 6¼
6½ 7
7¾ 8⅛
21¼ 22½
back
13 13⅜
18½ 20
6 6¼
10½ 11¼
left front
9¼ 10
6 6¼
16 16¾
sleeves
17¼ 17½
10 10¾

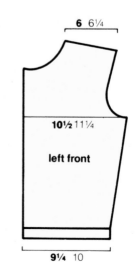

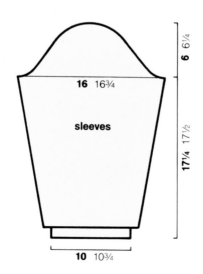

*floral nostalgia*

every foll 6th row 6 times.

*At same time,* keep front edge straight until work measures 18⅛ (18⅞) in, 46 (48) cm, from beg, ending at front edge.

▦ **Shoulder and Neck Shaping** Cast off 5 (6) sts at beg of next row, 2 sts at same edge on next 6 alt rows and 1 st on next 3 alt rows; *at same time,* after last inc at armhole edge, keep this edge straight until work matches back to shoulder, ending at this edge. Cast off 9 sts at beg of next row and next 2 alt rows, work 1 row then cast off rem 9 (11) sts.

### RIGHT FRONT

▦ Work as for left front until welt is completed then change to size 3 needles and cont on 56 (60) sts in st st working patt from Chart No 2.

▦ *1st row* K 1 (3) **A**, then working from chart k 23 **A**, join on **B** and k 1 **B**, k 31 **A** to complete chart, k 0 (2) **A**. Cont as now set and using Chart No 2 throughout, complete as for left front reversing shapings.

### LEFT SLEEVE

▦ With size 1 needles and **A** cast on 57 (61) sts and work in rib for same number of rows as on back welt but working 4 incs evenly spaced along last row. 61 (65) sts. Change to size 3 needles and beg with a k row work in st st; inc 1 st at both ends of every foll 8th row twice then work 0 (2) rows on these 65 (69) sts. **✻✻✻✻** Now work in patt from Chart No 1.

▦ *1st row* K 5 (7) **A** then working from chart k 31 **A**, join on **B**, k 1 **B**, then k 23 **A** to complete chart, then 5 (7) **A**. Cont as now set and work 6 (4) rows without shaping then inc at both ends of next row, then every foll 8th row 3 (4) times, then every foll 6th row 12 (11) times keeping all extra sts at sides in **A**. Cont on 97 (101) sts until work measures 17 (17⅜) in, 43 (44) cm, from beg.

▦ **Top Shaping** Cast off 2 sts at beg of next 10 rows, 1 st at beg of next 24 (26) rows, 2 sts at beg of next 12 rows and 3 sts at beg of next 2 rows. Cast off rem 23 (25) sts.

### RIGHT SLEEVE

▦ Work as for left sleeve to **✻✻✻✻** then work in patt from Chart No 2.

▦ *1st row* K 5 (7) **A**, then working from chart k 23 **A**, join on **B** and k 1 **B**, then k 31 **A** to complete chart then 5 (7) **A**. Cont as now set and complete to match left sleeve but using Chart No 2 throughout.

### FRONT BORDERS

▦ With size 2 needles and **A** cast on 11 sts and work in m st.

▦ *1st row* K 1, * p 1, k 1; rep from * to end; this row forms m st and all rows are alike. Cont until work measures 1¼ in (3 cm) from beg, then make buttonhole.

▦ *Next row* M st 4, cast off 3, m st to end. On foll row cast on 3 sts over buttonhole. Cont in m st making 3 more buttonholes each 5⅜ (5½) in, 13.5 (14) cm, above lower edge of previous one then cont until border when slightly stretched fits along front edge of right front. Cast off. Make similar border for left front omitting buttonholes.

### NECK BORDER

▦ With size 2 needles and **A** cast on 11 sts and work in m st for 33 (33¾) in, 84 (86) cm. Cast off.

### MAKING UP

▦ First complete the motifs by working the leaves in the Swiss Darning method described on page 6. Join shoulder seams. Sew in sleeves gathering in fullness at the top. Join side and sleeve seams. Sew on front borders stretching them slightly to fit. Matching center of neck border to center back sew border around neck edges beg and ending halfway across front borders leaving same length free at each end to tie. Sew on buttons to correspond with buttonholes.

*To achieve the authentic 1940s look, with wide shoulders to accentuate the cinched-in waist and demure tie neck, you should ideally insert shoulder pads, though these may be omitted if preferred. If you are using them, choose soft pads to avoid a rigid outline, catch-stitching them in place around the seams.*

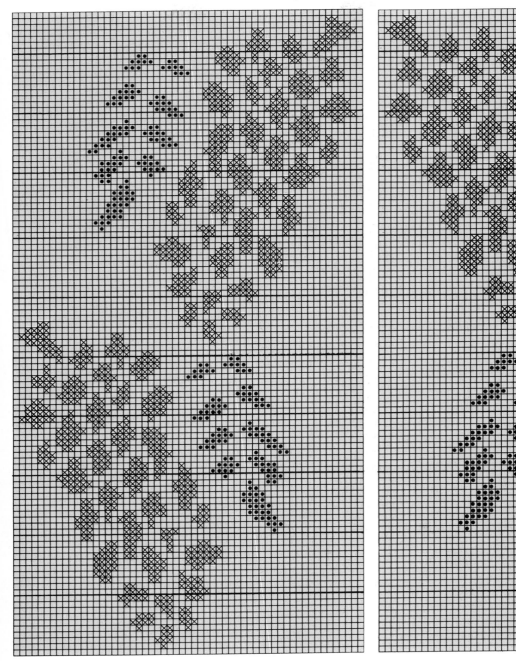

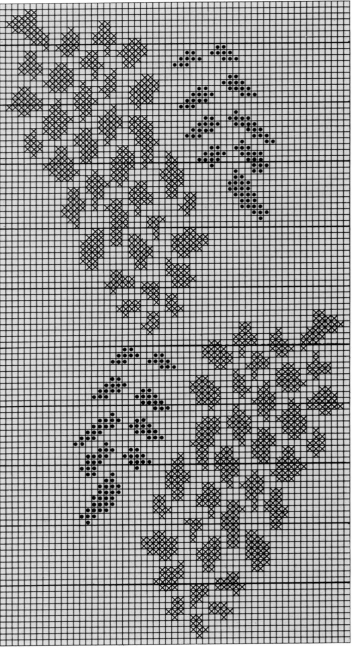

**KEY**

× Mauve

● Green

□ Gray

Chart 1 is used for the back, left front and left sleeve. Chart 2, which is a mirror image of Chart 1, is used for the right front and right sleeve. The mauve wisteria flowers are knitted in with the pattern while the leaves are added on later in Swiss darning (see page 6). Although the contrast between the knitted and embroidered areas of the motifs adds subtly to the texture of the pattern, you could knit the entire cardigan in the background shade and embroider the flowers as well as the leaves.

# ETHNIC AFRICA

Tribal patterns and sizzling tropical colors are used for two sweaters based on traditional African textile designs. Every decorative surface in a tribal culture has a symbolic significance. This feeling has been echoed in the knitting by enriching the shapes with long straight stitch, in black, and little knots of bright yellow in the black borders. Both sweaters are generous in fit, in line with the bold coloring and distinctive designs.

## CHECKLIST

### Materials
Pernelle Touareg: for Style 1, yellow as main color, 9 balls No 252 (**Y**), and 4 balls noir No 207 (**B**). For Style 2, black as main color, 8 balls noir No 207 (**B**), and 5 balls No 252 (**Y**). Pair each of needles size 2 and 3.
**Note** If the above yarn is unobtainable, refer to pages 78-9.

### Sizes
One size, to fit bust 36/40 in (92/102 cm), fitting very loosely. Actual measurements shown on diagram.

### Stitches used
Single rib; st st; patt, worked from charts. Separate balls are used for the various sections; take care always to twist them around each other when changing color.
Style 1 Use a separate ball for each of the large diamonds and triangles and small balls for the small triangles in **Y**; for the small triangles in **B** at top of chart wind a short length onto a piece of card for each motif. The darning is worked afterwards.
Style 2 Use separate balls of **B** and **Y** for the vertical panels and small balls of each for the elongated diamonds. The ball of **B** used for the large diamond is also used for the small center diamond. Join on short lengths of **B** for each of the small triangles; the spot in **Y** is worked afterwards. The single vertical lines in **B** are worked afterwards as is the darning.

### Tension
Over st st using size 3 needles, 24 sts and 32 rows to 4 in (10 cm). Work a sample on 30 sts.

## INSTRUCTIONS: STYLE 1

### BACK
▦ With size 2 needles and **Y** cast on 135 sts and work in rib.
▦ *1st row* (right side). P 1, * k 1, p 1; rep from * to end.
▦ *2nd row* K 1, * p 1, k 1; rep from * to end. Rep these 2 rows until work measures 3⅛ in (8 cm) from beg, ending with a 1st rib row.
▦ *Inc row* Rib 9, [inc in next st, rib 12] 9 times, inc in next st, rib 8. 145 sts. Change to size 3 needles and beg with a k row work in st st. Cont until work measures 8¼ in (21 cm) from beg, ending with a p row then begin working from Chart 1.

▦ *1st row* K 42 **Y**, join on a ball of **B**, k 1 **B**, then k 59 **Y**, join on another ball of **B**, k 1 **B**, then k 42 **Y**. Cont with colors as now set for 2 more rows.
▦ *4th row* P 41 **Y**, 3 **B**, 57 **Y**, 3 **B**, 41 **Y**. Cont with colors as now set for 2 more rows. Now join on separate balls of **Y** for the sections on each side of the triangles.
▦ *7th row* K 40 **Y**, 5 **B**, join on another ball of **Y**, k 55 **Y**, 5 **B**, join on another ball of **Y**, k 40 **Y**. Cont with colors as now set for 2 more rows. Now join on small balls of **Y** for centers of the triangles.
▦ *10th row* P 39 **Y**, 3 **B**, join on small ball of **Y**, 1 **Y**, 3 **B**, 53 **Y**, 3 **B**

# bold sweaters, tribal patterns

join on small ball of **Y**, 1 **Y**, 3 **B**, 39 **Y**. Cont for 2 more rows.

▦ *13th row* K 12 **Y**, rep from ⁎ to ⁎ on chart twice, joining on balls of **B** as required, 1 **B**, 12 **Y**. Cont working from chart, without shaping until 58th row of chart has been worked.

▦ **Armhole Shaping** Keeping patt correct cast off 4 sts at beg of next 2 rows, 3 sts at beg of next 4 rows and 2 sts at beg of next 2 rows then dec 1 st at both ends of every alt row 5 times. Cont on rem 111 sts until chart is completed then cont with **Y** only until work measures 26 in (66 cm) from beg, ending with a p row.

▦ **Neck Shaping** *1st row* K 40 and leave these sts of right back on needle, cast off 31, k to end. Cont on 40 sts now rem at end of needle for left back and work 1 row. Cast off 5 sts at beg of next row and next alt row, p 1 row on rem 30 sts, then cast off these sts for shoulder edge. Rejoin yarn to neck edge of right back sts, cast off 5, p to end. Cast off 5 sts at neck edge on next alt row, work 2 rows straight. Cast off rem 30 sts.

## FRONT

▦ Work as for back until work measures 23⅝ in (60 cm) from beg, ending with a p row.

▦ **Neck Shaping** *1st row* K 45 and leave these sts of left front on a spare needle, cast off next 21 sts,

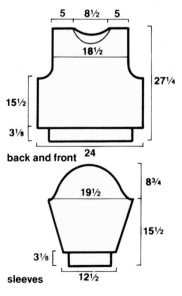

back and front

sleeves

k to end. Cont on 45 sts now rem on needle for right front and work 1 row straight. ✳✳ Cast off 4 sts at beg of next row, 2 sts at same edge on next 2 alt rows and 1 st on next 7 alt rows. Cont on rem 30 sts until work matches back to shoulder edge. Cast off. Rejoin yarn to neck edge of left front sts and complete as for right front from ✳✳ to end.

## SLEEVES

🔲 With size 2 needles and **Y** cast on 65 sts and work in rib as on back welt for 3⅛ in (8 cm) ending with a 1st rib row.

🔲 *Inc row* Rib 5, [inc in next st, rib 5] 10 times. 75 sts. Change to size 3 needles and beg with a k row work in st st but inc 1 st at both ends of every foll 6th row 8 times, then every foll 4th row 11 times. *At same time*, when 40 rows have been worked in st st and there are 87 sts, begin working from chart.

🔲 *1st row of chart* K 13 **Y**, join on a ball of **B**, k 1 **B**, then 59 **Y**, join on another ball of **B**, 1 **B**, then 13 **Y**. Cont working from chart as now set and cont with incs until all are completed taking extra sts into patt. Cont on 113 sts until 58th row has been worked from chart.

🔲 **Top Shaping** Keep patt correct until chart is completed then cont with **Y** only; cast off 4 sts at beg of next 2 rows, 3 sts at beg of next 4 rows and 2 sts at beg of next 2 rows; dec 1 st at both ends of every alt row 26 times, then cast off 2 sts at beg of next 10 rows and 3 sts at beg of next 2 rows. Cast off rem 11 sts.

## EMBROIDERY

🔲 Using a length of **B** threaded in a tapestry needle complete the patt by working vertical sts as shown on chart, taking care to alternate the positions of sts in each row to give the effect of darning.

## MAKING UP AND NECK BORDER

🔲 Join right shoulder seam. With right side of work facing and using size 2 needles and **Y**, pick up and k 78 sts around front neck edge and 55 sts across back neck. Beg with 2nd row work in rib for 9 rows then cast off loosely ribwise. Join left shoulder seam and ends of neck border. Sew in sleeves then join side and sleeve seams matching patt.

## INSTRUCTIONS: STYLE 2

### BACK

🔲 Using **B** instead of **Y**, work as for Style 1 until work measures 8¼ in (21 cm) from beg, ending with a p row then begin working from Chart 2.

🔲 *1st row* K 16 **Y**, ✳ join on a ball of **B**, k 5 **B**, join on another ball of **Y**, k 31 **Y**;✳ rep from ✳ to ✳ twice more, join on a ball of **B**, k 5 **B**, join on a ball of **Y**, k 16 **Y**. Now begin the small triangles in **B** joining on a

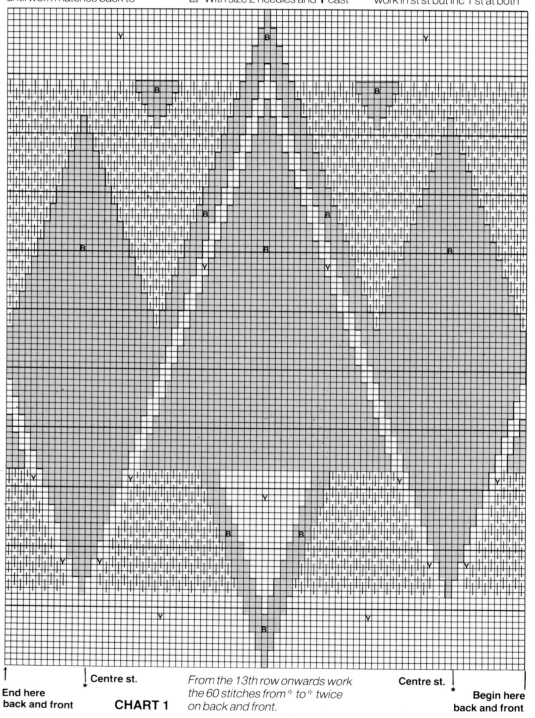

**End here**
**back and front**

| Centre st.

**CHART 1**

*From the 13th row onwards work the 60 stitches from ✳ to ✳ twice on back and front.*

Centre st. |

**Begin here**
**back and front**

short length of **B** for each, using the balls previously joined on for remainder of row.

⊞ *2nd row* P 12 **Y**, join on short length of **B**, p 1 **B**, then p 3 **Y**, * 5 **B**, 3 **Y**, join on short length of **B**, p 1 **B**, then 23 **Y**, join on short length of **B**, p 1 **B**, then 3 **Y**, * rep from * to * twice more, 5 **B**, 3 **Y**, join on short length of **B**, p 1 **B**, then 12 **Y**. Cont working from chart as now set and when 58th row has been worked, work armhole shaping as for Style 1. Cont on rem 111 sts until chart is completed then cont with **B** only and complete back as for Style 1.

## FRONT

⊞ Work as for back until chart is completed then cont with **B** only until work measures 23⅝ in (60 cm) from beg, ending with a p row. Complete as for front of Style 1.

## SLEEVES

⊞ Using **B** instead of **Y** work as for Style 1 until 40 rows have been worked and there are 87 sts. Now begin working from Chart 2.

⊞ *1st row of chart* K 23 **Y**, rep from * to * in 1st row given for back once, join on a ball of **B**, k 5 **B**, join on a ball of **Y**, k 23 **Y**. Cont in patt as now set and cont with incs until all are completed. Cont on 113 sts until 58th row has been worked from chart.

⊞ **Top Shaping** Keep patt correct until chart is completed then cont with **B**, only.

*At same time* shape top as for Style 1.

## EMBROIDERY

⊞ Using **Y** make a French knot in center of each of the small **B** triangles. Using a length of **B** threaded into a tapestry needle work the vertical sts as shown on chart to form the darning effect. Using **B** work the single vertical lines; on each side of the 5 sts in **B**, miss the next st in **Y** then cover the next st with a line of **B** using the Swiss Darning method.

## MAKING UP AND NECK BORDER

⊞ As for Style 1 using **B** for neck border.

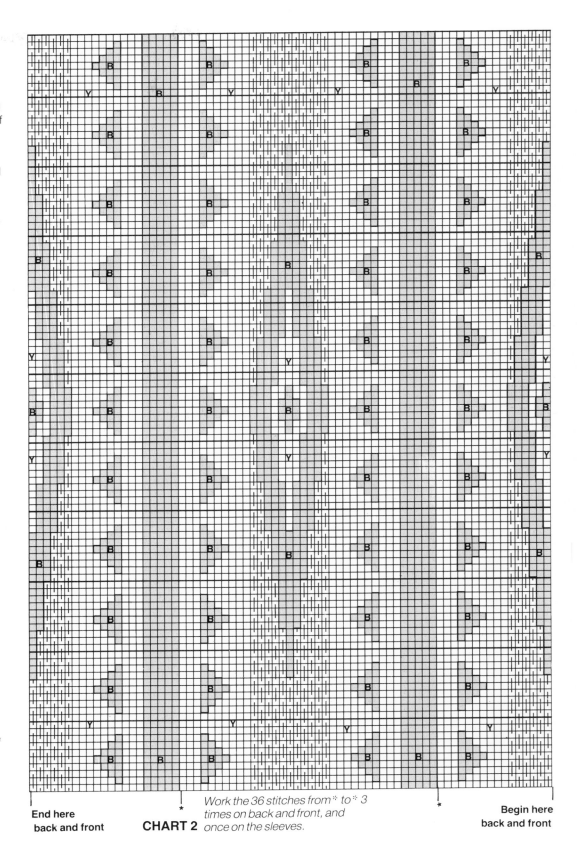

End here
back and front

**CHART 2**

*Work the 36 stitches from * to * 3 times on back and front, and once on the sleeves.*

Begin here
back and front

# CINEMASCOPE JERSEY

Cinemascope colors on a black background give great style to this big, loose-cut jersey, with raglan shaping. The two designs on the front of the sweater are knitted in, but the one on the sleeve is appliquéd on top of the finished sleeve seam for a neater effect. Filmic sprocket holes are embroidered on the stocking stitch after making up, a witty detail that is simplicity itself to achieve, and if you do not enjoy jacquard knitting you could Swiss darn all details.

## CHECKLIST

### Materials

*La Droguerie quality* Surnaturelle *in the foll colors: 9 (10) balls noir (**A**) and 1 ball chaudron (**5**), a dark tan shade; for the rem colors only small amounts are needed and in each case we give the shade name and also the actual color. Small amounts in anis (pale green), abricot (light orange), ocre (ochre), bleu ocean (deep blue), porcelaine (lighter blue), gris argent (silvery gray), saumon (salmon pink), bois de rose (deep pink), mangue (orange), jaune (yellow) and blanc (white). Pair each of needles size 0 and 2.*
**Note** *If the above yarn is unobtainable, refer to pages 78-9.*

### Sizes

*Two sizes, to fit bust 32/34 in (36/38) in; 82/87 (92/97) cm, fitting very loosely. Actual measurements shown on diagram.*

### Stitches used

*Single rib; st st; for the motifs work from charts as explained below. Use a separate ball of **A** for the sts on each side of the motifs and when **A** is used during the motif join on a short length to avoid carrying it across. Always twist yarns around each other when changing color. Join on the other colors as required. The short vertical lines around the yoke are embroidered on afterwards.*

### Tension

*Over st st using size 2 needles, 30 sts and 38 rows to 4 in (10cm). Work a sample on 36 sts.*

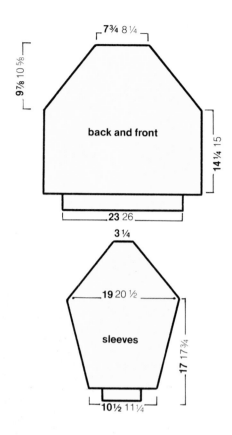

## INSTRUCTIONS

### BACK

▥ With size 0 needles and **A** cast on 159 (175) sts and work in rib.
▥ *1st row* (right side). P 1, * k 1, p 1; rep from * to end.
▥ *2nd row* K 1, * p 1, k 1; rep from * to end. Rep these 2 rows 7 times more then change to **5** and work 3 more rows. Change back to **A**.
▥ *Inc row* Rib 4 (2), [inc in next st, rib 9] 15 (17) times, inc in next st, rib 4 (2). 175 (193) sts. Change to size 2 needles and beg with a k row work in st st. Cont until work measures 5½ (6¼) in, 14 (16) cm, from beg, ending with a p row then begin motif from Chart A.
▥ *1st row* K 16 (22) **A**, join on

white and k 1, then k rem 74 sts of this chart in **A**, then k rem sts of row in **A**. On foll row join on a ball of pale green for background of chart leaving the first ball of **A** hanging at side of motif, joining on another ball of **A** for sts at other side. Remember always to twist **A** around the color being used for motif at beg and end of motif. When this motif is completed cont with **A** only until work measures 14⅛ (15⅜) in, 36 (39) cm, from beg, ending with a p row.
▥ **Raglan Shaping** Cast off 2 sts at beg of next 2 rows. ** K 1 row without shaping, dec at both ends of next 2 rows, p 1 row without shaping then dec at both ends of foll 2 rows. ** Rep from ** to ** 8

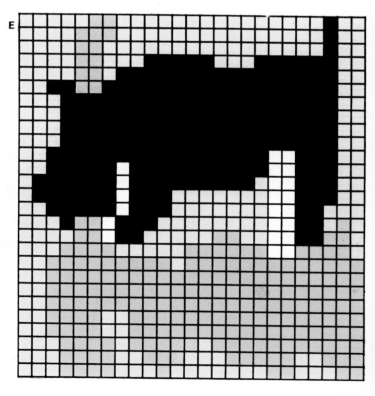

*jungle scenes on filmic black*

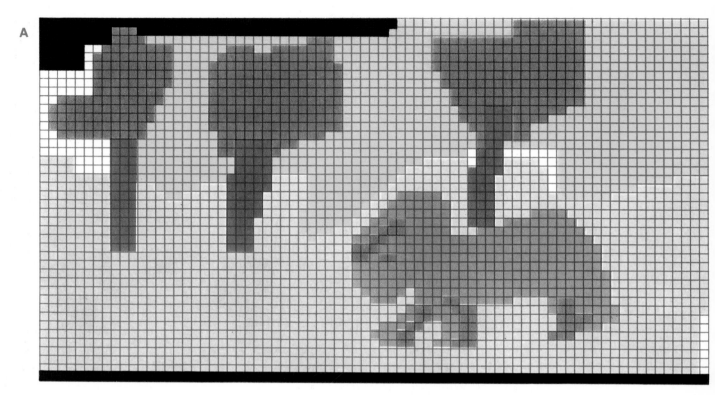

(12) times more. Now dec at both ends of every alt row 20 (11) times. Cast off rem 59 (63) sts for back neck.

## FRONT

▦ Work as for back until work measures 4 (4¾) in, 10 (12) cm, from beg, ending with a p row. Now begin motif from Chart B.

▦ *1st row* K 19 (25) **A**, then working from chart k 24 **A**, join on deep blue and k 11 sts with this, join on another ball of **A** and k rem 11 sts of motif then k rem sts of row in **A**. Cont working from chart as now set until motif is completed then work 4 rows in **A**. Now work motif from Chart C.

▦ *1st row* K 93 (105) **A**, join on pale green and k 41 with this, join on a short length of **A** and k 3, k 1 with the green, 3 **A**, then with green k rem 8 sts of motif, join on another ball of **A**, k 26 (32) **A**. Cont with this motif as now set and when it is completed cont with **A** only. Work as given for back, beg raglan shaping in same way and cont until 84 (90) rows of raglan shaping have been worked ending with a p row. 71 (75) sts.

▦ **Neck Shaping** *1st row* K 26 and leave these sts of left front on a spare needle, cast off next 19 (23) sts, k to end. Cont on 26 sts now rem on needle for right front. ✳✳✳ Cont to dec at raglan edge on next row and next 5 alt rows; *at same time* cast off at neck edge on alt rows 4 sts twice and 3 sts 3 times. After last raglan dec cast off rem 3 sts. Rejoin yarn to neck edge of left front sts and complete as for right front from ✳✳✳ to end.

## LEFT SLEEVE

▦ With size 0 needles and **A** cast on 69 (73) sts and work in rib as on back welt working 16 rows in **A** then 3 rows in **5**. Change back to **A**.

▦ *Inc row* Rib 4 (6), [inc in next st, rib 5 (4)] 10 (12) times, inc in next st, rib 4 (6). 80 (86) sts. Change to size 2 needles and beg with a k row work in st st using **A**. Inc 1 st at both ends of every foll 6th row 4 (2) times, then every foll 4th row 28 (33) times.

*At same time*, when work measures 15 (15¾) in, 38 (40) cm, from beg, ending with a p row, begin motif from Chart D on the

center 24 sts of row. When side incs are completed cont on 144 (156) sts until work measures 17 (17¾) in, 43 (45) cm, from beg, ending with a p row.

▦ **Raglan Shaping** Cont with motif until it is completed then cont in **A** and *at same time*, cast off 2 sts at beg of next 2 rows then rep from ✳✳ to ✳✳ as on back raglan 10 (13) times, then dec 1 st at both ends of every alt row 17 (11) times. Cast off rem 26 sts.

## RIGHT SLEEVE

▦ Work as for left sleeve but omitting the motif which is worked separately. For the motif cast on 25 sts using yellow and p 1 row then cont in st st working from Chart E with colors as shown.

## MAKING UP AND NECK BORDER

▦ Join front raglan seams and right back seam. With right side of work facing and using size 0 needles and **A**, pick up and k 25 sts across top edge of left sleeve, 71 (75) sts round front neck edge, 24 sts across top of right sleeve and 59 (63) sts across back neck.

Beg with 2nd row work in rib as on welt working 13 rows in **A**, 3 rows in **5** and 16 rows in **A**. Cast off loosely ribwise. Join left shoulder seam and ends of neck border. Now using white work the short vertical lines beg on front. Mark the center st of work at a position 3⅛ in (8 cm) above start of raglan and using the Swiss Darning method explained on page 6, cover this st in white and work 9 more sts above this in a vertical line. Miss next 9 sts to one side and work a similar line, then cont in this way to raglan edge. Work similar lines on other side of center and cont the lines across each sleeve forming a neat angle where the lines meet on raglan.

▦ Join side and sleeve seams. Slip-st motif worked from Chart E to right sleeve with lower edge 5⅛ (5⅞) in, 13 (15) cm, from beg of sleeve and placing it exactly centered over sleeve seam. Fold neck border in half to wrong side and slip-st cast-off edge to back of picked-up sts.

**A** *Back*
**B** *Left front*
**C** *Right front*
**D** *Left sleeve*
**E** *(see page 28) Right sleeve*
**A, B, C** *and* **D** *are knitted in with the pattern.* **E** *is Swiss darned (see page 6) after the sleeve seam has been sewn.*

**KEY**

 **1** *Pale green*

**2** *Apricot/orange*

**3** *Ochre*

**4** *Deep blue*

**5** *Tan*

**6** *Porcelain/mid-blue*

**7** *Silvery grey*

**8** *Salmon*

**9** *Old rose*

**10** *Peachy-sand*

**11** *Golden yellow*

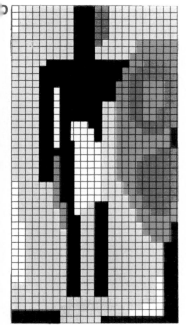

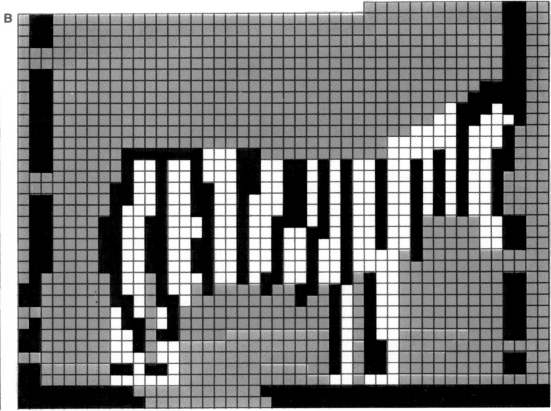

# TECHNICOLOR MOHAIR

This beautiful drop-sleeve coat uses all the colors of the primary palette to give drama to plain black. The main sections are worked with a strand each of thick yarn and mohair twined together, for thickness and luxury. Under the mohair coat is a dazzling red mini with a huge roll collar and turnback cuffs in a different, thick, fluffy yarn. The main parts are in a wide rib, with a fisherman's rib for the collar and cuffs. Large needles make both quick to knit.

## MULTICOLORED COAT

## CHECKLIST

### Materials

*La Droguerie Mohair: 500g noir (**A**). Surnaturelle: 350g noir (**B**). Benjamine: 160g rouge vermillon (**C**), bright red; 50g blue dur (**E**), bright blue; 50g jaune (**J**), yellow; 50g violet (**G**); 50g vert vif (**H**), bright green; 100g fuchsia (**D**), and 50g orange (**F**). Pair each of needles size 5 and 7; a cable needle; 2 buttons.*
**Note** *If the above yarn is unobtainable, refer to pages 78-9.*

### Sizes

*Two sizes, to fit bust 32/34 (36/38) in; 82/87 (92/97) cm. Actual measurements shown on diagram; these measurements do not include the cable braids.*

### Stitches used

Rice st, *worked on an odd number of sts as folls:*
  1st row *(right side).* K 1, * p 1, k 1; rep from * to end.
  2nd row *K all sts. These 2 rows form one patt.*
  Cable patt *worked over 13 sts for the braids.*
  1st row *(right side). P 2, k 9, p 2.*
  2nd row *P all sts.*
  3rd row *P 2, slip next 3 sts on cable needle, leave at back, k 3, then k 3 from cable needle, k next 3 sts, p 2.*
  4th row *P.*
  5th row *P 2, k 3, slip next 3 sts on cable needle, leave at front, k 3, then k 3 from cable needle, p 2.*
  6th row *P. The last 4 rows from 3rd to 6th inclusive, form one patt.*

### Tensions

*Over rice st using size 7 needles and a strand each of **A** and **B** tog, 18 sts and 24 rows to 4 in (10 cm). The braid worked on size 5 needles using Pingofrance, measures 1 ½ in (4 cm) wide.*

## INSTRUCTIONS

### BACK

▦ With size 7 needles and using **A** and **B** tog cast on 91 (103) sts and work in rice st; cont until work measures 27½ (29½) in, 70 (75) cm from beg, ending with a 2nd patt row. Cast off all sts in patt. On cast-off edge mark the center 33 (37) sts for neckline leaving 29 (33) sts on each side for shoulders.

### LEFT FRONT

▦ With size 7 needles and using **A** and **B** tog, cast on 49 (55) sts and work in rice st; cont until work measures 24⅜ (26⅜) in, 62 (67) cm, from beg, ending with a 1st patt row.
▦ **Neck Shaping** Cast off 12 (14) sts at beg of next row, 2 sts at same edge on next 2 alt rows and 1 st on next 4 alt rows. ** Cont on rem 29 (33) sts until work

*black and brilliant*

measures 27½ (29½) in, 70 (75) cm, from beg, ending with a 2nd patt row. Cast off in patt.

### RIGHT FRONT

▦ With size 7 needles and using **A** and **B** tog, cast on 57 (63) sts and work in rice st; cont until work measures 24⅜ (26⅜) in, 62 (67) cm, from beg, ending with a 2nd patt row.

▦ **Neck Shaping** Cast off 20 (22) sts at beg of next row, 2 sts at same edge on next 2 alt rows and 1 st on next 4 alt rows. Complete as for left front from ** to end.

### SLEEVES

▦ Each sleeve is worked in two halves. For one half cast on 17 (19) sts using size 7 needles and **A** and **B** tog. Work 4 rows in patt then to shape side edge inc 1 st at beg of next row, then at same edge on every foll 4th row 6 times more, then on every alt row 34 (36) times working extra sts into patt. Cont on 58 (62) sts until work measures 17 (17¾) in, 43 (45) cm, from beg, ending with a 2nd patt row.

▦ Cast off in patt. Work other half of sleeve in same way but working shapings at opposite edge – end of right-side rows.

### POCKET

▦ Make one only. With size 7 needles and using **A** and **B** tog, cast on 39 (41) sts and work in patt for 9 (9½) in, 23 (24) cm, ending with a 2nd patt row. Cast off in patt.

### BRAIDS

▦ These are all worked with size 5 needles; cast on 13 sts for each braid and work in cable patt using colors as folls: using **C** work a braid 15 (16⅛) in, 38 (41) cm long for sewing between right front and back and a similar braid using **D** for sewing between left front and back. Using **H** work a braid 17 (17¾) in, 43 (45) cm long for center of left sleeve and a similar braid using **J** for center of right sleeve. Using **H** work a braid 6¼ (7) in, 16 (18) cm long for left shoulder and a similar braid using **J** for right shoulder. Using **D** work a braid 26⅜ (30) in, 67 (71) cm long for left armhole and a similar braid using

**C** for right armhole. Using **F** work a braid 24⅜ (26⅜) in, 62 (67) cm long for left front border and a similar braid using **E** for right front border. Using **G** work a braid 22½ (24⅜) in, 57 (62) cm long for neck border; leave the sts of this braid on a safety pin for adjustment if necessary without cutting yarn. Using **F** work a braid long enough to fit across top of pocket.

### MAKING UP

▦ Sew shoulder braids between shoulder edges of back and front; for all the braids lap edge of braid over edge of main part and sew in place with small neat sts in the purl edging. Assemble the two halves of each sleeve by sewing the braids between them. Sew armhole borders to upper edges of each sleeve ensuring that when seen from the front the braid patt will run vertically on each armhole. Pin other edge of armhole borders to sides of coat matching center of sleeve to center of shoulder braid and ensuring that 15 (16⅛) in, 38 (41) cm, is left free on each side edge. Sew armhole borders in place; join sleeve seams and cont seams along half the width of armhole borders. Now sew side braids between side edges of back and fronts and sew rem edges of armhole borders to top edge of side braids. Sew pocket braid to top of pocket and slip-st pocket to right front in desired position. Sew on front borders. Starting at right front neck edge pin neck border all around neck edges; adjust length if necessary so that it ends at left front neck edge and cast off sts. Sew neck border in place. Lap right front over left, sew a button to left front neck border and make a buttonhole loop on right front edge to correspond. Make another loop on front edge of left front border and sew rem button to wrong side of right front neck to correspond.

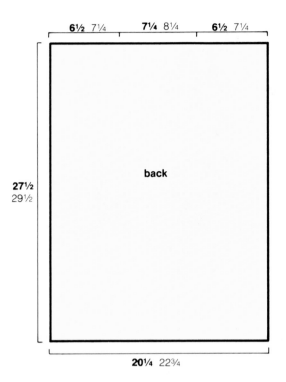

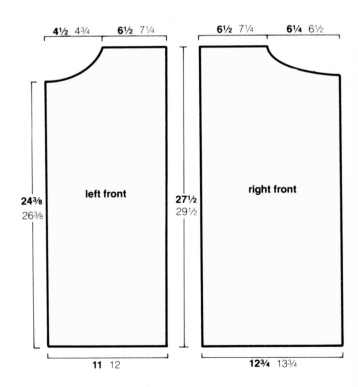

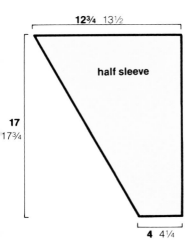

12¾ 13½

**half sleeve**

17
17¾

4 4¼

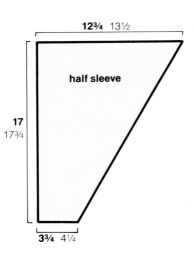

12¾ 13½

**half sleeve**

17
17¾

3¾ 4¼

*The measurements given above do not include the 1½in (4cm) wide cable pattern braids. These are used to join the back to fronts at the shoulders and down the sides, to join the two halves of each sleeve down the top seam and to attach the sleeves to the body of the coat. Braids are also used to give a decorative edging to the fronts, neck and pockets.*

## ROLL COLLAR DRESS

## CHECKLIST

### Materials
*La Droguerie* Mohair: 650g rouge. Pair each of needles size 5 and 7.
**Note** *If the above yarn is unobtainable, refer to pages 78-9.*

### Sizes
*Two sizes, to fit bust 32/34 (36/38) in; 82/87 (92/97) cm. Actual measurements shown on diagram.*

### Stitches used
Wide rib patt, *worked on a multiple of 10 sts plus 3 as folls:*
1st row *(right side)*. P 4, * p 5, k 5; rep from * to last 9 sts, p 5, k 4.
*2nd row k 4, * p 5, k 5; rep from * to last 9 sts, p 5, k 4. These 2 rows form patt. Fisherman rib, worked on an even number of sts as folls:*
1st row *(right side)*. K all sts; this row forms a foundation and is not worked again.
2nd row K 1, * k next st but in row below, inserting needle through work from front to back and allowing st above to drop off needle, k next st normally; rep from * to last st, k 1. This row forms patt; cont to rep 2nd row throughout. The rib effect does not appear until several rows have been worked.

### Tensions
*Over wide rib patt using size 7 needles and flattening work slightly when measuring, 19 sts and 22 rows to 4 in (10cm). Over Fisherman rib patt using size 5 needles, 15 sts and 32 rows to 4 in (10cm). When counting rows in this patt each k rib which you can see counts as 2 rows.*

## INSTRUCTIONS

### MAIN PART
▦ Beg at lower edge of back cast on 103 (113) sts and work in wide rib patt. Cont until work measures 20⅞ (22½) in, 53 (57)cm, from beg, ending with a 2nd patt row.

▦ **Sleeve Shaping** Cast on 2 sts at beg of next 10 (6) rows and 3 sts at beg of next 36 (40) rows taking extra sts into patt. 231 (245) sts. The right-side rows will now begin and end k 3 (5) and wrong-side rows p 3 (5). At this point it may be more convenient to use a circular needle still working in rows as usual. Cont in patt and work 4¾

(5⅛) in, 12 (13) cm, without shaping ending with a wrong-side row.

▦ **Neck Shaping** *1st row* Patt 100 (106) and leave these sts of right back on a spare needle, cast off next 31 (33) sts in patt, then patt to end.
Cont on 100 (106) sts now rem on needle for left back. ** Dec 1 st at neck edge on next 4 rows. The shoulder line has now been reached so place a marker loop of contrast yarn at side edge and cont on same sts for left front. Work 2 in (5 cm) without shaping on rem 96 (102) sts ending at neck edge. Inc 1 st at beg of next row

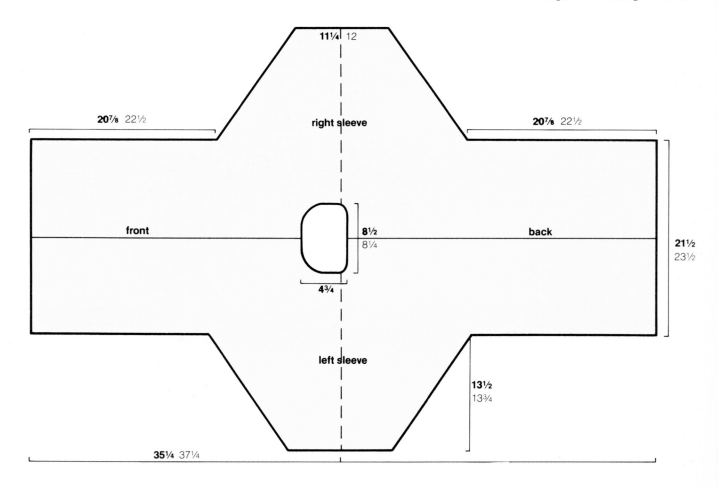

and next 2 alt rows then cast on 2 sts at same edge on next 2 alt rows and 4 sts on next alt row. ✻✻ Work 1 row on these 107 (113) sts thus ending at neck edge then cut yarn and leave these sts on a spare needle.

▦ Rejoin yarn to neck edge of right back sts and cont as for left back and front from ✻✻ to ✻✻ ending at side edge after last shaping row.

▦ *Next row* Patt across these 107 (113) sts, turn, cast on 17 (19) sts, turn, then work in patt across sts of left front. 231 (245) sts. Cont in patt across all sts until work measures 5½ (5⅞) in, 14 (15) cm from shoulder markers, ending with a wrong-side row.

▦ **Sleeve Shaping** Cast off 3 sts at beg of next 36 (40) rows and 2 sts at beg of next 10 (6) rows. Cont on rem 103 (113) sts and work 20⅞ (22½) in, 53 (57) cm, in patt. Cast off loosely in patt.

## COLLAR

▦ With size 5 needles cast on 126 (130) sts and work in Fisherman rib; cont until work measures 9½ in (24 cm) from beg. Cast off very loosely.

## CUFFS

▦ Make 2 alike. With size 5 needles cast on 42 (44) sts and work in Fisherman rib patt until work measures 6⅝ in (17 cm) from beg. Cast off very loosely.

## MAKING UP

▦ With right side of cuff to wrong side of dress sew cast-off edges of cuffs to side edges of sleeve sections of main part. Join side and sleeve seams reversing seams on cuffs. Join sides of collar. With right side of collar to wrong side of dress, placing seam at center back, sew cast-off edge of collar to neck edges easing in collar to fit.

*The roll collar dress is the perfect partner for the coat featured on the previous page, but you could easily shorten the pattern to make a chunky sweater. The dress is knitted in one piece, like a poncho but with added cuffs and collar.*

# JAPANESE WAVE

Inspired by the Japanese artist, Hokusai, this all-weather pullover can be worn with winter woollens or over lighter-weight summer skirts. The back of the design is worked in stripes to echo the colors of the waves and foam. It's much less complicated than it first appears – graphs give you all the decorative details, and stocking stitch is easy to maintain.

## CHECKLIST

### Materials
*Laine Marigold 4 fils using the foll colors: 5 balls marine No 8601 (**1**), blue black; 3 balls ecru No 8627 (**7**); 2 balls mélé gris moyen No 8650 (**4**), mid gray; 2 balls mélé gris No 8607 (**3**), light gray; 2 balls granit bleu No 8691 (**2**), blue gray; 1 ball or part-ball in each of the foll, berlingot No 8798 (**5**), pink; terre No 8804 (**6**), mid brown; hussard No 8739 (**11**), light blue; ciel No 8097 (**12**), darker blue; opaline No 8811 (**13**), light green; bleu roi No 8616 (**9**), royal blue; porcelaine No 8693 (**8**), bright blue, and marmara No 8674 (**10**), dark blue green. Pair each of needles size 2 and 4.*
**Note** *If the above yarn is unobtainable, refer to page 78.*

### Size
*One size to fit bust 32/36 in (82/92 cm). Actual measurements given on diagram.*

### Stitches used
*Single rib; st st; patt, worked from charts on front and sleeves. Use separate balls or short lengths of yarn for each of the sections shown on chart taking care to wind yarns around each other when changing color. Any very small sections can be embroidered on afterwards using the Swiss Darning method described on page 6. Back is worked in stripes to coincide with some of the color changes on the front.*

### Tension
*Over st st using Laine Marigold and size 4 needles or Pingouin yarns and size 3 needles, 24 sts and 32 rows to 4 in (10 cm). Work a sample on 28 sts. Take care to use the stated sizes for the correct yarn.*

## INSTRUCTIONS

### BACK
With smaller needles and **1** cast on 115 sts and work in rib.
*1st row* (right side). P 1, * k 1, p 1; rep from * to end.
*2nd row* K 1, * p 1, k 1; rep from * to end. Rep these 2 rows until work measures 3⅛ in (8 cm) from beg, ending with a 1st rib row.
*Inc row* Rib 9, [inc in next st, rib 15] 6 times, inc in next st, rib 9. 122 sts. Change to larger needles and beg with a k row work in st st. Work 74 rows in **1**, 6 rows in **4**, 32 rows in **3** and 24 rows in **2**, then cont with **1**.
*At same time*, cont until 98 rows have been worked in st st.

**Armhole Shaping.** Cast off 4 sts at beg of next 2 rows, 2 sts at beg of next 6 rows and 1 st at beg of next 4 rows. Cont on rem 98 sts and when the stripe in **2** has been completed cont with **1** until 156th row has been worked in st st.

**Neck and Shoulder Shaping**
*157th row* K 36 and leave these sts of right back on spare needle, cast off next 26 sts, k to end. Cont on 36 sts now rem on needle for left back and work 1 row straight.
** Cast off 3 sts at beg of next row and 10 sts at side edge on foll row; rep last 2 rows once. Work 1 row straight then cast off rem 10 sts to complete shoulder slope. Rejoin yarn to neck edge of right back sts and complete as for left back from

*oceanic blues and grays*

**FRONT**

▦ Work as for back until the inc row has been completed at end of welt. Change to larger needles and beg with a k row work in st st working patt from Chart 1. Work armhole shaping as given for back beg on 99th row of chart. Cont on rem 98 sts until 137th row has been worked from chart.

▦ **Neck and Shoulder Shaping**
*138th row* Patt 43 and leave these sts of right front on a spare needle, cast off next 12 sts, patt to end. Cont on 43 sts now rem on needle for left front and work 1 row straight. ✳✳✳ Cast off 3 sts at beg of next row, 2 sts at same edge on next 2 alt rows and 1 st on next 6 alt rows. ✳✳✳ Cont on rem 30 sts and work 2 rows straight then cast off for shoulder 10 sts at beg of next row and next alt row, work 1 row then cast off rem 10 sts.

▦ Rejoin yarn to neck edge of right front sts and keeping patt correct cont as for left front from ✳✳✳ to ✳✳✳. Cont on rem 30 sts until 159th row has been worked from chart thus ending at side edge. Shape shoulder as for left front.

**RIGHT SLEEVE**

▦ With smaller needles and **1** cast on 53 sts and work in rib as on back welt for 2¾ in (7 cm), ending with a 1st rib row.

▦ *Inc row* Rib 1, [inc in next st, rib 4] 10 times, inc in next st, rib 1. 64 sts. Change to larger needles and beg with a k row work in st st working patt from Chart 2. Inc 1 st at both ends of 5th row, then every foll 4th row 3 times, then at both ends of every foll 6th row 7 times, then every foll 8th row 4 times. All these incs are shown on chart. Cont on 94 sts until 128 rows have been worked from chart.

▦ **Top Shaping** Cast off 4 sts at beg of next 2 rows and 2 sts at beg of next 8 rows; now dec 1 st at both ends of every alt row 8 times, then cast off 2 sts at beg of next 12 rows and 3 sts at beg of next 6 rows. Cast off rem 12 sts.

**LEFT SLEEVE**

▦ Work as for right sleeve but working patt from Chart 3.

**NECK BORDER**

▦ Join right shoulder seam. With right side of work facing and using smaller needles and **1**, pick up and k 57 sts around front neck edge and 42 sts across back neck. Beg with 2nd row work in rib for 6 rows then cast off loosely ribwise.

**MAKING UP**

▦ Join left shoulder seam and ends of neck border. Sew in sleeves. Join remaining seams.

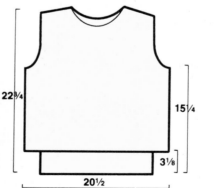

back and front

*If you find the fine detail of the huge tsunami wave too daunting to knit, many of the isolated splashes of foam could easily be Swiss darned after the larger-scale areas have been knitted.*

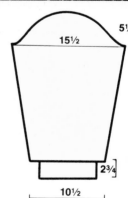

sleeves

*Note that although the neck and shoulder shapings are shown on the chart as being at both ends of the same row, they are worked at the start of consecutive rows in the usual manner.*

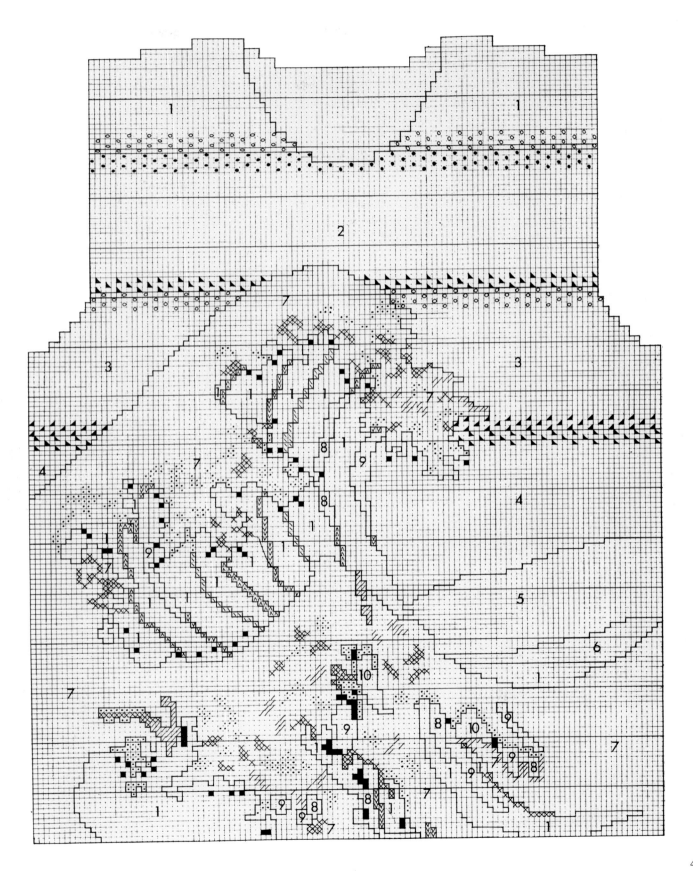

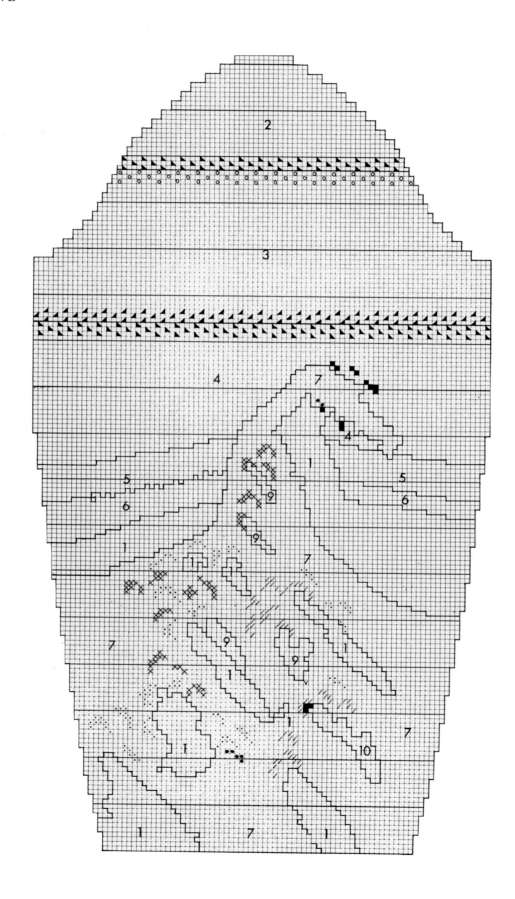

**KEY**

**1 and** ● *Blue black*
**2 and** ○ *Blue gray*
**3 and** ◣ *Light gray*
**4 and** ◥ *Mid gray*
**5** *Pink*
**6** *Mid brown*
**7 and** ■ *Ecru*
**8 and** ⌃ *Bright blue*
**9 and** ⌄ *Royal blue*
**10 and** ` *Dark blue green*
**11 and** . *Light blue*
**12 and** × *Darker blue*
**13 and** / *Light green*

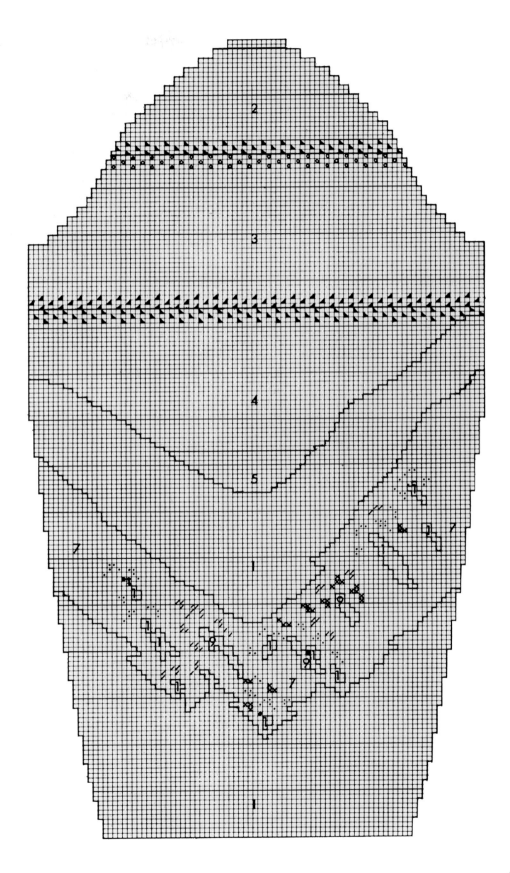

*The subtle effect of the finished sweater is due in large part to the use of closely related shades in a limited color range of blues, grays and neutrals, with just a touch of brown and green. The colors available in different yarns are constantly changing and it may not be possible for you to use exactly the same shades as the designer, but provided you keep to a similar palette of colors there is no reason why your sweater should not be just as successful as the original. As with the front, the sleeve top shapings are shown on the charts as being at both ends of the same row but they are made at the beginning of consecutive rows in the usual manner.*

# THIRTIES FAVORITES

Create an echo of the past with 1930s lacy patterns in a classic T-shirt line. All four are the same shape and all are knitted in a pure cotton yarn for a cool, summery feel. You need a little experience for the laces, which all have delightfully old-fashioned names. The first, in pale blue, is called the 'bunch of grapes' pattern. The second, in a darker blue, is known as 'the waffle', while the third, very French in ecru, is called 'fantasy zig-zag lace'. The fourth, a nostalgic old-rose pink, is called 'dance of the little faun'. Intricate lace patterns can be time-consuming to knit, but these little T-shirts are worked on large needles so they do not take an age to make.

## BUNCH OF GRAPES

## CHECKLIST

### Materials
*Georges Picaud Akala mercerized cotton: 8 (9-9) balls. Pair each of needles size 2 and 6.*

### Sizes
*Three sizes, to fit bust 30/32 (34-36/38) in; 76/82 (87-92/97) cm. Actual measurements shown on diagram.*

### Stitches used
Single rib; g st; bunch of grapes patt, *worked on a multiple of 8 sts plus 2 as folls:*

1st row *K 1, \* yfd, k 1 tbl, yfd, SKPO, k 5; \* rep from \* to \* ending k 1.*
2nd row *P 1, \* p 4, p 2 tog tbl, p 3; \* rep from \* to \* ending p 1.*
3rd row *K 1, \* yfd, k 1 tbl, yfd, k 2, SKPO, k 3; \* rep from \* to \*, ending k 1.*
4th row *P 1, \* p 2, p 2 tog tbl, p 5; \* rep from \* to \* ending p 1.*
5th row *K 1, \* k 1 tbl, yfd, k 4, SKPO, k 1, yfd; \* rep from \* to \*, ending k 1.*
6th row *P 1, \* p 1, p 2 tog tbl, p 6; \* rep from \* to \* ending p 1.*
7th row *K 1, \* k 5, k 2 tog, yfd, k 1 tbl, yfd; \* rep from \* to \* ending k 1.*
8th row *P 1, \* p 3, p 2 tog, p 4; \* rep from \* to \* ending p 1.*
9th row *K 1, \* k 3, k 2 tog, k 2, yfd, k 1 tbl, yfd; \* rep from \* to \* ending k 1.*
10th row *P 1, \* p 5, p 2 tog, p 2; \* rep from \* to \* ending p 1.*
11th row *K 1, \* yfd, k 1, k 2 tog, k 4, yfd, k 1 tbl; \* rep from \* to \* ending k 1.*
12th row *P 1, \* p 6, p 2 tog, p 1; \* rep from \* to \* ending p 1.*
*These 12 rows form one patt. This patt requires some care; where the patt rep ends with yfd as on 5th, 7th and 9th rows remember to work the yfd at end of row before the last k 1. On every right-side row an extra st is made in each patt rep and these are eliminated on the foll row. If counting sts after a right-side row count the sts of each rep as 8 sts; do not make an extra yfd in places where you will be casting off on foll row.*

### Tension
*Over patt using size 6 needles, 20 sts and 24 rows to 4 in (10 cm). Work a sample on 26 sts; this should measure 5⅛ in (13 cm) wide.*

*classic T-shirt shapes in lace*

## INSTRUCTIONS

### BACK

▦ With size 2 needles cast on 90 (98-106) sts and work in g st for 3 rows then change to size 6 needles and work in patt as given above. Cont until work measures 16⅛ (16½-17) in, 41 (42-43) cm, from beg, ending with a wrong-side row.

▦ **Armhole Shaping** Cast off 4 sts at beg of next 2 rows and 2 sts at beg of next 2 rows then dec 1 st at both ends of next 2 alt rows. Cont on rem 74 (82-90) sts until work measures 24⅜ (25¼-26) in, 62 (64-66) cm from beg, ending with a wrong-side row.

▦ **Shoulder and Neck Shaping** Cast off 6 (7-8) sts at beg of next 2 rows.

▦ *Next row* Cast off 6 (7-8), patt until there are 11 (12-13) sts on right needle, leave these for right back, cast off next 28 (30-32) sts, patt to end. Cont on 17 (19-21) sts now rem at end of needle for left back. Cast off 6 (7-8) sts at beg of next row and 4 sts at neck edge on foll row. Cast off rem 7 (8-9) sts to complete shoulder slope. Rejoin yarn to neck edge of right back sts, cast off 4, patt to end. Cast off rem 7 (8-9) sts.

### FRONT

▦ Work as for back until work measures 22 (22⅞-23⅝) in, 56 (58-60) cm, from beg, ending with a wrong-side row.

▦ **Neck and Shoulder Shaping** *Next row* Patt 32 (35-38) and leave these sts of left front on a spare needle, cast off next 10 (12-14) sts, patt to end.

Cont on 32 (35-38) sts now rem on needle for right front and work 1 row. ✳✳ Cast off 4 sts at beg of next row, 2 sts at same edge on next 3 alt rows and 1 st on next 3 alt rows. *At same time*, when work matches back to beg of shoulder, ending at side, cast off 6 (7-8) sts at beg of next row and next alt row, work 1 row then cast off rem 7 (8-9) sts.

▦ Rejoin yarn to neck edge of left front sts; complete as for right front from ✳✳ to end.

### SLEEVES

▦ With size 2 needles cast on 70 (74-78) sts and work 2 rows in g st then k 1 more row working 4 incs evenly spaced. 74 (78-82) sts. Change to size 6 needles and patt; for 1st and 3rd sizes work patt as given above. (For 2nd size work 2 extra sts in st st at each side; thus the right-side rows will begin and end k 3 and wrong-side rows p 3.) Cont in patt until work measures 2 in (5 cm) from beg then inc 1 st at both ends of next row keeping this extra st at each side in st st. Cont on 76 (80-84) sts until work measures 3⅛ (3⅛-3½) in, 8 (8-9) cm, from beg, ending with a wrong-side row.

▦ **Top Shaping** Cast off 4 sts at beg of next 2 rows, 2 sts at beg of next 8 (10-12) rows, 4 sts at beg of next 6 rows and 8 sts at beg of next 2 rows. Cast off rem 12 sts.

### NECK BORDER

▦ Join right shoulder seam. With right side of work facing and using size 2 needles, pick up and k 57 (59-61) sts around front neck edge and 38 (40-42) sts across back neck.

▦ *1st row* (wrong side). K 1, * p 1, k 1; rep from * to end.

▦ *2nd row* P 1, * k 1, p 1; rep from * to end. Cast off loosely ribwise.

### MAKING Up

▦ Join left shoulder seam and ends of neck border. Sew in sleeves then join side and sleeve seams.

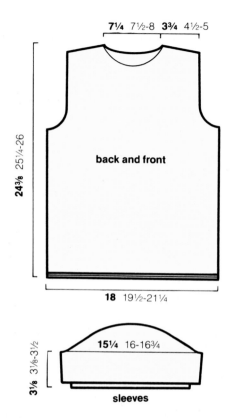

7¼  7½-8  3¾  4½-5

24⅜ 25¼-26

**back and front**

18  19½-21¼

3⅛ 3⅛-3½  15¼  16-16¾

**sleeves**

## THE WAFFLE
## CHECKLIST

### Materials

*Filature de Paris Big Louisiana: 10 (11-11) balls gobelin, or color of your choice. Pair each of needles size 2 and 6.*
**Note** *If the above yarn is unobtainable, refer to pages 78-9.*

### Sizes

*Three sizes, to fit bust 32/34 (36-38) in; 82/87 (92-97) cm. Actual measurements shown on diagram.*

### Stitches used

Single rib; g st; cross 2 = *pass needle in front of 1st st, lift up 2nd st and k it leaving it on needle, then k 1st st and slip both off needle;* yo2 = *wind yarn twice around right needle;* k 2 in loop = *drop one loop of the yo2 to make a long st and k into front then into back of this st;* waffle patt, *worked on a multiple of 4 sts plus 2 as folls:*

1st row *(right side).* K 1, yfd, * SKPO, k 2 tog, yo2; rep from * to last 5 sts, SKPO, k 2 tog, yfd, k 1.
2nd row K 2, * p 2, k 2 in loop; rep from * to last 4 sts, p 2, k 2.
3rd row K 1, p 1, * cross 2, p 2; rep from * to last 4 sts, cross 2, p 1, k 1.
4th row K 2, * p 2, k 2; rep from * to end.
5th row K 1, * k 2 tog, yo2, SKPO; rep from * to last st, k 1.
6th row K 1, p 1, * k 2 in loop, p 2; rep from * ending last rep p 1, k 1.
7th row K 2, * p 2, cross 2; rep from * to last 4 sts, p 2, k 2.
8th row K 1, p 1, * k 2, p 2; rep from * to last 4 sts, k 2, p 1, k 1.
*These 8 rows form one patt.*

## Tension

*Over patt using size 6 needles, 22 sts and 25 rows to 4 in (10 cm). Work a sample on 26 sts.*

## INSTRUCTIONS

### BACK

▦ With size 2 needles cast on 102 (110-118) sts and work 3 rows in g st then change to size 6 needles and work in patt as given above. Cont until work measures 16⅛ (16½-17) in, 41 (42-43) cm, from beg, ending with a wrong-side row.

▦ **Armhole Shaping** Cast off 4 sts at beg of next 2 rows and 2 sts at beg of next 2 rows then dec 1 st at both ends of next 2 alt rows. Cont on rem 86 (94-102) sts until work measures 24⅜ (25¼-26) in, 62 (64-66) cm, from beg, ending with a wrong-side row.

▦ **Shoulder and Neck Shaping** Cast off 8 sts at beg of next 2 rows.

▦ *Next row* Cast off 8, patt until there are 11 (14-17) sts on right needle, leave these for right back, cast off next 32 (34-36) sts, patt to end. Cont on 19 (22-25) sts now rem at end of needle for left back. Cast off 8 sts at beg of next row

and 4 sts at neck edge on foll row. Cast off rem 7 (10-13) sts to complete shoulder slope. Rejoin yarn to neck edge of right back sts, cast off 4, patt to end. Cast off rem 7 (10-13) sts.

### FRONT

▦ Work as for back until work measures 22 (22⅞-26) in, 56 (58-60) cm, from beg, ending with a wrong-side row.

▦ **Neck and Shoulder Shaping** *Next row* Patt 38 (41-44) and leave these sts of left front on a spare needle, cast off next 10 (12-14) sts, patt to end. Cont on 38 (41-44) sts now rem on needle for right front and work 1 row straight. ** Cast off 4 sts at beg of next row and next alt row, 2 sts at same edge on next 2 alt rows and 1 st on next 3 alt rows.

*At same time*, keep side edge straight until work matches back to shoulder, ending at side then cast off 8 sts at beg of next row and next alt row, work 1 row then

cast off rem 7 (10-13) sts. Rejoin yarn to neck edge of left front sts and complete as for right front from ** to end.

### SLEEVES

▦ With size 2 needles cast on 77 (81-85) sts and work 2 rows in g st then k 1 more row working 5 incs evenly spaced. 82 (86-90) sts. Change to size 6 needles and work in patt; cont until work measures 2 in (5 cm) from beg then inc 1 st at both ends of next row. Keep extra st at each side in st st still with border st in g st as before. Cont on 84 (88-92) sts until work measures 3⅛ (3⅛-3½) in, 8 (8-9) cm, from beg, ending with a wrong-side row.

▦ **Top Shaping** Cast off 4 sts at beg of next 2 rows, 3 sts at beg of next 2 rows, 2 sts at beg of next 8 (10-12) rows, 4 sts at beg of next 6 rows and 8 sts at beg of next 2 rows. Cast off rem 14 sts.

### NECK BORDER

▦ Join right shoulder seam, backstitching this and all seams. Press all seams lightly on wrong side with warm iron and damp cloth avoiding ribbing and g st.

With right side of work facing and using size 2 needles, pick up and k 57 (59-61) sts round front neck edge and 38 (40-42) sts across back neck.

▦ *1st row* (wrong side). K 1, * p 1, k 1; rep from * to end.

▦ *2nd row* P 1, * k 1, p 1; rep from * to end. Cast off loosely ribwise.

### MAKING UP

▦ Join left shoulder seam and ends of neck border. Sew in sleeves then join side and sleeve seams.

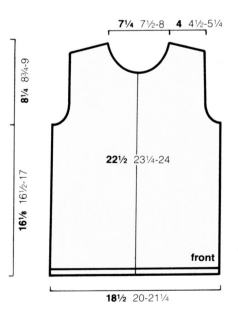

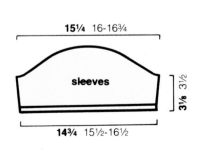

| | | | | |
|---|---|---|---|---|
| 4 | 4½-5¼ | 7¼ | 7½-8 | |

8¼  8¾-9

25¼  26-26¾

16⅛  16½-17

**back**

18½  20-21¼

7¼  7½-8    4  4½-5¼

22½  23¼-24

**front**

18½  20-21¼

15¼  16-16¾

**sleeves**

3⅛  3½

14¾  15½-16½

## DANCE OF THE LITTLE FAUN

## CHECKLIST

### Materials

*Georges Picaud* Akala *mercerized cotton: 8 (9) balls. Pair each of needles size 2 and 6.*

### Sizes

*Two sizes, to fit bust 30/32 (34/36) in; 76/82 (87/92) cm. Actual measurements shown on diagram.*

### Stitches used

Single rib; g st; dance of the little fawn patt, *worked on a multiple of 12 sts plus 3 as folls:*

  1st row *K 2, * SKPO, k 3, yfd, k 1, yfd, k 3, k 2 tog, k 1; * rep from * to * ending k 1.*
  2nd row *P 2, * p 2 tog, p 2, yrn, p 3, yrn, p 2, p 2 tog tbl, p 1; * rep from * to * ending p 1.*
  3rd row *K 2, * SKPO, k 1, yfd, k 5, yfd, k 1, k 2 tog, k 1; * rep from * to * ending k 1.*
  4th row *P 2, * yrn, p 2 tog, p 7, p 2 tog tbl, yrn, p 1; * rep from * to * ending p 1.*
  5th row *K 2, * yfd, k 3, k 2 tog, k 1, SKPO, k 3, yfd, k 1; * rep from * to * ending k 1.*
  6th row *P 3, * yrn, p 2, p 2 tog tbl, p 1, p 2 tog, p 2, yrn, p 3; * rep from * to *.*
  7th row *K 4, * yfd, k 1, k 2 tog, k 1, SKPO, k 1, yfd, k 5; * rep from * but ending last rep k 4 instead of k 5.*
  8th row *P 5, * p 2 tog tbl, yrn, p 1, yrn, p 2 tog, p 7; * rep from * to * but ending last rep k 5, instead of k 7.*
*These 8 rows form one patt.*

### Tension

*Over patt using size 6 needles, 20 sts and 26 rows to 4 in (10 cm). Work a sample on 27 sts.*

## INSTRUCTIONS

### BACK

▦ With size 2 needles cast on 87 (99) sts and work 4 rows in g st then change to 4½ mm needles and work in patt. Cont until work measures 16⅛ (17) in, 41 (43) cm, from beg, ending with a wrong-side row.

▦ **Armhole Shaping** Cast off 3 sts at beg of next 2 rows and 2 sts at beg of next 2 rows then dec 1 st at both ends of next alt row. 75 (87) sts. A half-patt has been taken off at each side; if the next row to be worked is a 1st patt row then the 5th row should be worked and this will fit correctly, if the next row is a 3rd row then the 7th row will fit correctly and so on. Cont thus in patt until work measures 24⅜ (25⅝) in, 62 (65) cm, from beg, ending with a wrong-side row.

▦ **Shoulder and Neck Shaping** Cast off 6 sts at beg of next 2 rows.
▦ *Next row* Cast off 6, patt until there are 11 (15) sts on right needle, leave these for right back, cast off next 29 (33) sts, patt to end. Cont on 17 (21) sts now rem at end of needle for left back. Cast off 6 sts at beg of next row and 4 sts at neck edge on foll row. Cast off rem 7 (11) sts to complete shoulder slope.
▦ Rejoin yarn to neck edge of right back sts, cast off 4, patt to end. Cast off rem 7 (11) sts.

### FRONT

▦ Work as for back until work measures 22 (23¼) in, 56 (59) cm, from beg, ending with a wrong-side row.

▦ **Neck and Shoulder Shaping**
*Next row* Patt 32 (36) and leave these sts of left front on a spare

needle, cast off next 11 (15) sts, patt to end. Cont on 32 (36) sts now rem on needle for right front and work 1 row. ** Cast off 4 sts at beg of next row 2 sts at same edge on next 3 alt rows and 1 st at same edge on next 3 alt rows.
*At same time,* when work matches back to beg of shoulder, ending at side, cast off 6 sts at beg of next row and next alt row, work 1 row then cast off rem 7 (11) sts.
▦ Rejoin yarn to neck edge of left front sts; complete as for right front from ** to end.

### SLEEVES

▦ With size 2 needles cast on 70 (74) sts and work 3 rows in g st then k 1 more row working 5 incs evenly spaced. 75 (79) sts. Change to size 6 needles and work in patt; for 1st size work rows as given above. (For 2nd size work 2 extra sts in st st at each side; thus the 1st patt row will begin and end k 4, the 2nd row will begin and end p 4, and so on).
Cont in patt until work measures 2 in (5 cm) from beg then inc 1 st at both ends of row keeping the extra st each side in st st.
Cont on 77 (81) sts until work measures 3⅛ (3½) in, 8 (9) cm, from beg, ending with a wrong-side row.
▦ **Top Shaping** Cast off 3 sts at beg of next 2 rows, 2 sts at beg of next 10 (12) rows, 4 sts at beg of

next 6 rows and 6 sts at beg of next 2 rows. Cast off rem 15 sts.

### NECK BORDER

▦ Join right shoulder seam. With right side of work facing and using size 2 needles, pick up and k 58 (62) sts around front neck edge and 39 (43) sts across back neck.
▦ *1st row* (wrong side). K 1, * p 1, k 1; rep from * to end.
▦ *2nd row* P 1, * k 1, p 1; rep from * to end. Rep these 2 rows once then cast off loosely ribwise.

### MAKING UP

▦ Join left shoulder seam and ends of neck border. Sew in sleeves then join side and sleeve seams.

7½  8¼   3⅛  3½

24¾  26

**back and front**

17¼  19¾

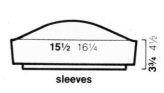

15½  16¼

3¾  4½

**sleeves**

## FANTASY ZIG-ZAG LACE

## CHECKLIST

### Materials
*Pingouin* Coton Naturel 8 fis: *10 (11) balls. Pair each of needles size 2 and 6.*

### Sizes
*Two sizes, to fit bust 32/34 (36/38) in; 82/87 (92/97) cm. Actual measurements shown on diagram.*

### Stitches used
Single rib; g st; zig-zag lace patt, *worked over a multiple of 9 sts plus 4 as folls:*

    1st row *(right side).* K 3, * yfd, k 1, yfd, k 2, k 2 tog tbl, k 2 tog, k 2; *rep from* * *to last st, k 1.*
    2nd row *P.*
    3rd to 10th rows *Rep 1st and 2nd rows 4 times more.*
    11th row *K 3,* * k 2 tog tbl, k 2 tog, k 2, yfd, k 1, yfd, k 2; *rep from* * *to last st, k 1.*
    12 row *P.*
    13th to 20th rows *Rep 1st and 2nd rows 4 times more. These 20 rows form one patt.*

### Tension
*Over patt using size 6 needles, 19 sts and 28 rows to 4 in (10 cm). Work a sample on 22 sts, changing needle size if necessary as explained on page 6.*
Note *The zig-zag patt causes the side edges to assume an irregular shape; to correct this, before making up garment pin out the sections onto an ironing board, gently pulling the sides so that they are straight and parallel. Lay a damp cloth on the work and press very lightly with a warm iron avoiding g st edgings. Leave in place until they are quite dry; this should be done before working neck border.*

## INSTRUCTIONS

### BACK
▦ With size 2 needles cast on 94 (103) sts and work 3 rows in g st. Change to size 6 needles and work in patt as given above. Cont until work measures 16⅛ (17) in, 41 (43) cm, from beg, ending with a p row.
▦ **Armhole Shaping** Cast off 4 sts at beg of next 2 rows and 2 sts at beg of next 2 rows then dec 1 st at both ends of next 3 alt rows. Cont on rem 76 (85) sts until work measures 24⅜ (25⅝) in, 62 (65) cm, from beg, ending with a p row.
▦ **Shoulder and Neck Shaping** Cast off 6 sts at beg of next 2 rows.
▦ *Next row* Cast off 6, patt until there are 18 (21) sts on right needle, leave these for right back, cast off next 16 (19) sts, patt to end.

Cont on 24 (27) sts now rem at end of needle for left back. Cast off 6 sts at beg of next row and 9 sts at neck edge on foll row. Cast off rem 9 (12) sts to complete shoulder slope.
▦ Rejoin yarn to neck edge of right back sts, cast off 9, p to end. Cast off rem 9 (12) sts.

### FRONT
▦ Work as for back until armhole shaping is completed then cont until work measures 22 (23¼) in, 56 (59) cm, from beg, ending with a p row.
▦ **Neck and Shoulder Shaping**
*Next row* Patt 32 (35) and leave these sts of left front on a spare needle, cast off next 12 (15) sts, patt to end.
Cont on 32 (35) sts now rem on needle for right front and work 1 row straight. ** Cast off 4 sts at beg of next row, 2 sts at same

edge on next 2 alt rows and 1 st on next 3 alt rows.
Work a few rows on rem 21 (24) sts until work matches back to shoulder, ending at side edge.
▦ Cast off 6 sts at beg of next row and next alt row, work 1 row then cast off rem 9 (12) sts.
▦ Rejoin yarn to neck edge of left front sts and complete as for right front from ** to end.

### SLEEVES
▦ With size 2 needles cast on 67 (71) sts and work 2 rows in g st then k 1 more row working 5 incs evenly spaced. 72 (76) sts. Change to size 6 needles and work in patt.
▦ For 1st size, rows will read as folls: On either 1st or 11th patt row begin k 1, then rep from * in correct patt row ending last rep with k 1 instead of k 2.
▦ For 2nd size, work the normal patt rows. Cont in patt without shaping until work measures 3⅛ (3½) in, 8 (9) cm, from beg, ending with a p row.
▦ **Top Shaping** Cast off 4 sts at beg of next 2 rows, 3 sts at beg of next 2 rows, 2 sts at beg of next 6 rows, 3 sts at beg of next 8 rows and 6 sts at beg of next 2 rows. Cast off rem 10 (14) sts.

### NECK BORDER
▦ Before working border press parts as explained above. Join right shoulder seam; press all seams in same way avoiding rib and g st. With right side facing and using size 2 needles, pick up and k 57 (60) sts round front neck edge and 38 (41) sts across back neck.
▦ *1st row* (wrong side). K 1, * p 1, k 1; rep from * to end.
▦ *2nd row* P 1, * k 1, p 1; rep from * to end. Rep these 2 rows once then cast off loosely ribwise.

### MAKING UP
▦ Join left shoulder seam and ends of neck border. Sew in sleeves. Join side and sleeve seams.

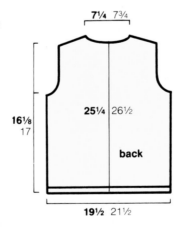

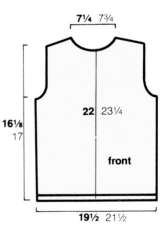

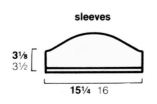

sleeves

# AT THE RUSSIAN BALLET

Leon Bakst set Paris on fire with his designs for the Russian Ballet in the 1910s. This gorgeous evening sweater is based on his distinctive ideas. The main blocks of the pattern are worked in glittering yarns and soft, fine wools, used double. Embroidery on top adds a brocaded opulence. The entire garment, front, sleeves and back, is knitted in one piece.

## CHECKLIST

### Materials

*Berger du Nord* Douceur: *8 balls noir No 8521 (1); 3 balls pinède No 8545 (6), jade; 3 balls rouge No 8532 (4), red; 2 balls lavande No 8539 (5), blue; 1 ball rosée No 8529, old rose, and 1 ball paille No 8532, pale yellow. Moonlight: 6 balls or No 6422 (2), gold, and 10 balls champagne No 7466 (3), pinky gold. Pair each of needles size 5 and 6.*
**Note** *If the above yarns are unobtainable, refer to pages 78-9.*

### Sizes

*Two sizes, to fit bust 32/34 (36/38) in; 82/87 (92/97) cm. Actual measurements shown on diagram.*

### Stitches used

*Single rib; st st; patt, worked from chart. The various sections indicated by numbers should be worked in the appropriate colors as shown in the key to chart. All unnumbered areas should be embroidered on after the knitting is complete, using the Swiss Darning method described on page 6.*
**Note** *Yarns are used double throughout; take a ball of the color, wind it into 2 equal balls then wind these tog to form a double thickness ball which is easier to use.*

### Tension

*Over st st using size 6 needles and yarn double, 19 sts and 28 rows to 4 in (10 cm). Work a sample on 24 sts.*

## INSTRUCTIONS

### MAIN PART

▦ Beg at lower edge of front cast on 79 (83) sts using size 5 needles and **1**. Work in rib as folls:
▦ *1st row* (right side). P 1, * k 1, p 1; rep from * to end.
▦ *2nd row* K 1, * p 1, k 1; rep from * to end. Rep these 2 rows until work measures 2⅜ in (6 cm) from beg, ending with a 2nd rib row.
▦ *Inc row* Rib 4 (3), [inc in next st, rib 2, inc in next st, rib 3] 10 (11) times, inc in next st, rib 4 (2). 100 (106) sts. Change to size 6 needles and p 1 row on wrong side.

Now work in st st beg with a k row and work from chart; join on balls of the various colors indicated for the backgrounds on which the motifs will be embroidered and always twist yarns around each

other when changing color. Cont until 68 rows have been worked.
▦ **Sleeve Shaping** Cast on 3 sts at beg of next 4 (0) rows and 6 sts at beg of next 26 (30) rows; begin working the small squares and triangles during these rows. When shapings are completed cont on these 268 (286) sts and work 42 rows without shaping; 140 rows have been worked from chart.
▦ **Neck Opening** *141st row* Patt 106 (115) and leave these sts of left shoulder section on a spare needle, now with **2**, p next 56 sts to make a ridge on right side for fold-line, turn and leave rem 106 (115) sts of right shoulder section on a spare needle. Cont on center 56 sts and beg with another p row work 6 rows in st st using **2** then cast off loosely. For back neck facing cast on 56 sts using **2**; beg

*a gala knit for great scenes*

with a k row work 6 rows in st st.

▦ *Next row* P these sts to make a ridge for foldline then onto same needle with right side facing work the 106 (115) sts which were left unworked thus competing 141st row.

▦ *142nd row* Patt 162 (171) then cont in patt across the first group of 106 (115) sts. Cont in patt across all sts for back; work 42 rows without shaping.

▦ **Sleeve Shaping** Cast off 6 sts at beg of next 26 (30) rows and 3 sts at beg of next 4 (0) rows. 100 (106) sts. Working patt to correspond with front work 68 rows without shaping. Cont with **1** only and k 1 row.

▦ *Dec row* P 4 (3), [p 2 tog, p 2, p 2 tog, p 3] 10 (11) times, p 2 tog, p 4 (2). Cont on rem 79 (83) sts; change to size 5 needles and work in rib as on front welt for 2⅜ in (6 cm). Cast off loosely ribwise.

**MAKING UP AND CUFFS**

▦ First embroider the various motifs as shown on chart. With right side of work facing and using size 5 needles and **2**, pick up and k 43 sts along outer edge of one sleeve. Beg with 2nd row work in rib for 2⅜ in (6 cm) then cast off loosely ribwise. Work other cuff in same way. Join entire side and sleeve seams. Fold neck facings to wrong side along the fold-lines and slip-st in place.

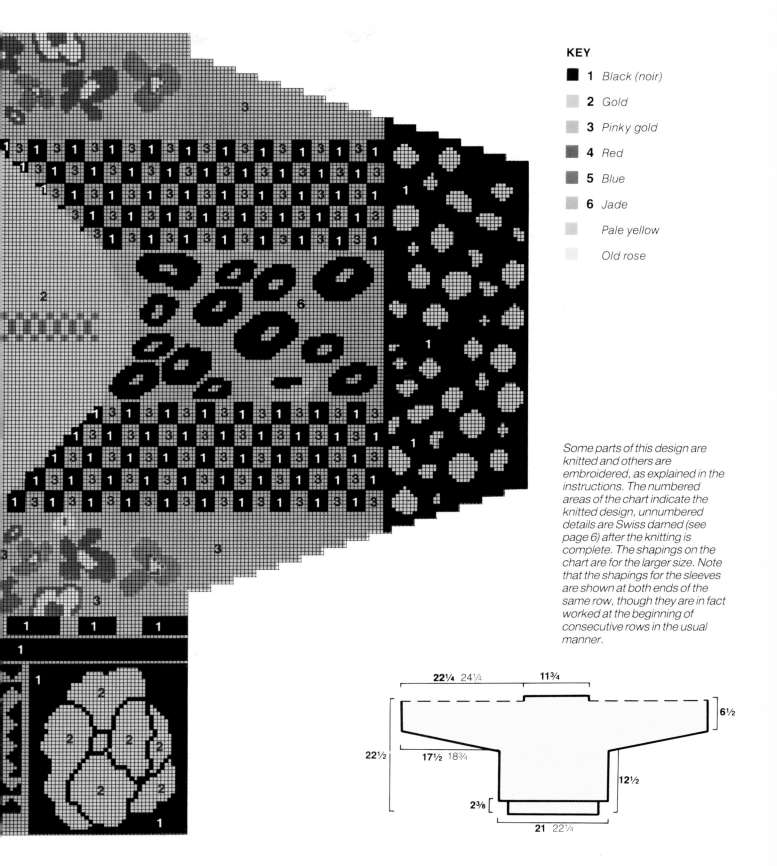

**KEY**

■ **1** Black (noir)

**2** Gold

**3** Pinky gold

**4** Red

**5** Blue

**6** Jade

Pale yellow

Old rose

Some parts of this design are knitted and others are embroidered, as explained in the instructions. The numbered areas of the chart indicate the knitted design, unnumbered details are Swiss darned (see page 6) after the knitting is complete. The shapings on the chart are for the larger size. Note that the shapings for the sleeves are shown at both ends of the same row, though they are in fact worked at the beginning of consecutive rows in the usual manner.

# GEOMETRICS FOR THE SHADE

These two geometric sweaters are the perfect cover-up for cooler summer days, or for the slight chill of evenings out of doors. They have a classic French elegance, but are new in styling, combining a loose fit with a short cut, sitting neatly on the hips. The cotton yarn is easy to handle – use separate balls for each block of color. Minimum shaping avoids complications: the back and front are mirror images, and the sleeves are simply reversed in coloring.

## TWO-COLOR PATTERN

## CHECKLIST

### Materials
*Phildar* Détente: *5 balls in white (1), and 5 balls indigo (2). Pair each of needles size 2 and 5.*

### Size
*One size, to fit bust 34/38 in; (87/97 cm). Actual measurements shown on diagram.*

### Stitches used
Single rib; st st; patt *on back and front, work from chart using a separate ball for each section. Always twist yarns around each other when changing color, picking up the new color from underneath the one previously used, to avoid leaving a hole. The patt on the sleeves is explained in the instructions.*

### Tension
*Over st st using size 5 needles, 20 sts and 26 rows to 10 cm (4 in). Work a sample on 26 sts, changing needle size if necessary as explained on page 6.*

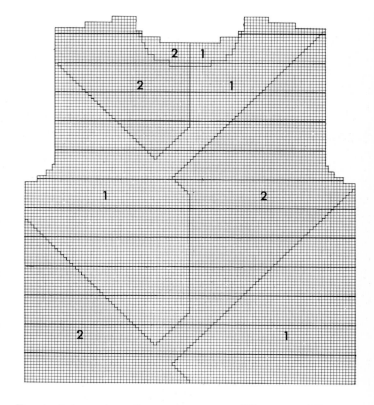

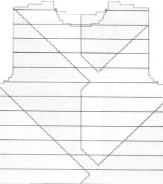

The chart above shows the arrangement of panels on the back of the two-color geometric sweater; read k rows from right to left and p rows from left to right. For the front see the smaller chart which shows the reverse arrangement of panels; read k rows from left to right and p rows from right to left.

## INSTRUCTIONS

### BACK
▨ With size 2 needles and **2** cast on 55 sts then using **1** cast on 55 sts onto same needle. 110 sts. Work in single rib, half in each color as folls:
▨ *1st row* (right side). With **1**, [k 1, p 1] 27 times, k 1, twist **2** around **1** and bring **2** to front then with **2** [p 1, k 1] 27 times, p 1.
▨ *2nd row* With **2**, [k 1, p 1] 27 times, k 1, bring **2** to front and twist **1** around it then with **1** [p 1, k 1] 27 times, p 1. Rep these 2 rows until work measures 2 in (5 cm) from beg, ending with a 2nd row then change to size 5 needles and work in st st work patt from chart.
▨ *1st row* K 55 **1**, twist yarns, 55 **2**.
▨ *2nd row* P 54 **2**, twist yarns, 56 **1**. Cont working from chart as now set until 66 rows have been worked.

▨ **Armhole Shaping** Cast off 4 sts at beg of next 2 rows; 3 sts at beg of next 2 rows; 2 sts at beg of next 2 rows and 1 st at beg of next 2 rows. Cont on rem 90 sts until 122 rows have been worked from chart. For remaining rows work sts of right half in **1** and left half in **2**.
▨ **Shoulder and Neck Shaping** *1st row* Cast off 10 sts, k until there are 25 sts on right needle, leave these for right back, cast off next 20 sts, k to end. Cont on 35 sts now rem at end of needle for left back. Cast off 10 sts at beg of next row and 6 sts at neck edge on foll row, then 9 sts for shoulder at beg of next row and 2 sts at neck edge on foll row. Cast off rem 8 sts to complete shoulder slope. Rejoin yarn to neck edge of right back sts, cast off 6, p to end. Cast off 9 sts at beg of next row and 2 sts at neck edge on foll row. Cast off rem 8 sts.

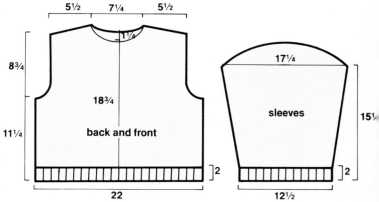

*simple cotton cover-ups*

### FRONT

▦ With size 2 needles and **1** cast on 55 sts then using **2** cast on 55 sts onto same needle. 110 sts.

▦ *1st row* With **2**, [k 1, p 1] 27 times, k 1, twist **1** around **2** then with **1**, [p 1, k 1] 27 times, p 1. Cont in rib as now set until same number of rows have been worked as on back welt.

▦ Change to size 5 needles and working in st st, work patt from chart reversing arrangement of colors. Work armhole shaping as given for back then cont on rem 90 sts until 110 rows have been worked from chart.

▦ **Neck and Shoulder Shaping**
*1st row* Keeping patt correct k 38 and leave these sts of left front on a spare needle, cast off next 14 sts, k to end. Cont on 38 sts now rem on needle for right front and work 1 row straight. ❖❖ Cast off 5 sts at beg of next row; 2 sts at same edge on next alt row and 1 st on next 4 alt rows.

▦ Now cast off for shoulder 10 sts at beg of next row, 9 sts at same edge on next alt row, work 1 row then cast off rem 8 sts.

▦ With wrong side facing rejoin **2** to neck edge of left front sts and complete as for right front from ❖❖ to end using **2** only.

### RIGHT SLEEVE

▦ With size 2 needles and **1** cast on 42 sts and work in single rib for 2 in (5 cm) ending with a wrong-side row. Change to size 5 needles.

▦ *Inc row* K 2 [kfb, k 1] 20 times. 62 sts. Beg with a p row cont in st st and work 6 rows straight then inc 1 st at both ends of next row; then every foll 8th row 4 times; then every foll 6th row 7 times. *At same time*, after 42 rows have been worked in st st and there are 72 sts begin **2** section at center.

▦ *43rd row* K 35 **1**, join on a ball of **2**, k 2 **2**, join on another ball of **1**, k 35 **1**. Twist yarns around each other when changing color as on other parts.

▦ *44th row* P 34 **1**, 4 **2**, 34 **1**. Cont working 2 extra sts in **2** at center on every row until all sts are in **2** and *at same time* after last inc row work 6 rows straight on 86 sts,

thus ending with a p row.

▦ **Top Shaping** Cast off 1 st at beg of next 4 rows; 2 sts at beg of next 4 rows; 3 sts at beg of next 4 rows; 2 sts at beg of next 4 rows; 4 sts at beg of next 4 rows and 9 sts at beg of next 2 rows. Cast off rem 20 sts.

### LEFT SLEEVE

▦ Work as for right sleeve but using **2**; cont until 32 rows have been worked in st st and there are 70 sts. Begin **1** section in center.

▦ *33rd row* K 34 **2**, join on **1** and k 2 **1**, join on another ball of **2**, k 34 **2**. Cont working 2 extra sts in **1** at center until all sts are in **1**. *At same time* cont as for right sleeve until shapings are completed then work 6 rows on 86 sts, ending with a p row.

▦ **Top Shaping** Cast off 1 st at beg of next 4 rows, 2 sts at beg of next 4 rows and 3 sts at beg of

next 4 rows. 62 sts. Now begin **2** section at center.

▦ *Next row* With **1**, cast off 2, k until there are 28 sts on right needle, join on **2**, k 2 **2**, then join on another ball of **1** and k rem 30 sts in **1**. Cont working 2 extra sts in **2** at center until all sts are in **2**. *At same time* complete shaping as for right sleeve.

### MAKING UP AND NECK BORDER

▦ Join right shoulder seam. Press all seams lightly on wrong side with warm iron and damp cloth. With right side of work facing and using size 2 needles and **1**, pick up and k 59 sts around front neck edge and 39 sts across back neck. Work in single rib for ¾ in (2 cm) then cast off loosely ribwise. Join left shoulder seam and ends of neck border. Sew in sleeves then join side and sleeve seams.

## THREE-COLOR PATTERN

## CHECKLIST

### Materials
*Pingouin* Corrida; *4 balls granit No 524* (**1**), *blue gray, 3 balls blanc No 501* (**2**), *and 3 balls noir No 528* (**3**). *Pair each of needles size 2 and 6.*

### Size
*One size, to fit bust 34/38 in; (87/97 cm). Actual measurements shown on diagram.*

### Stitches used
*Single rib; st st; for the* patt *on front and back work from chart using a separate ball for each section. Always twist yarns around each other on wrong side when changing color, picking up the new color from underneath the one previously used, to avoid leaving a hole.*

### Tension
*Over st st using size 6 needles, 19 sts and 26 rows to 4 in (10 cm). Work a sample on 25 sts, changing needle size if necessary as explained on page 6.*

## INSTRUCTIONS

### FRONT

▦ With size 2 needles and **2** cast on 52 sts then using **1** cast on 52 sts onto same needle. (104 sts). Work in single rib, half in each color as folls:

▦ *1st row* (right side). With **1**, [k 1, p 1] 26 times, take **1** to back and twist **2** around it, then with **2**, [k 1, p 1] 26 times.

▦ *2nd row* With **2**, [k 1, p 1] 26 times, bring **2** to front, twist **1** around it then with **1**, [k 1, p 1] 26 times.
Cont in rib as now set until work measures 2 in (5 cm) from beg, ending with a 2nd row. Change to size 6 needles and work in st st still with colors in same positions, working from chart.

▦ *1st row* K 52 **1**, twist yarns, 52 **2**. Cont as now set for 7 more

rows.

▦ *9th row* K 51 **1**, join on **3** and k 1 **3**, then 52 **2**. Cont in this way working from chart and beg new panels as shown, until 60th row has been worked from chart. The first panel of **1** has been eliminated.

▦ **Armhole Shaping** Cast off 3 sts at beg of next 4 rows; 2 sts at beg of next 2 rows; and 1 st at beg of next 4 rows. Cont on rem 84 sts until 106 rows have been worked from chart.

▦ **Neck and Shoulder Shaping**
*107th row* Patt 37 and leave these sts of left front on a spare needle, cast off next 10 sts, patt to end. Cont on 37 sts now rem on needle for right front and work 1 row straight. ** Cast off 4 sts at beg of next row and foll alt row, 2 sts at same edge on foll alt row and 1 st on foll alt row. Work 4 rows on rem 26 sts thus ending at side.

▦ Cast off for shoulder 10 sts at beg of next row and foll alt row, work 1 row then cast off rem 6 sts. Rejoin yarn to neck edge of left front sts and complete as for right front from ** to end keeping patt correct.

## BACK

▦ With size 2 needles and **1** cast on 52 sts then using **2** cast on 52 sts onto same needle. Work in single rib as foll:

▦ *1st row* (right side). With **2**, [k 1, p 1] 26 times, take **2** to back and twist **1** around it, then with **1**, [k 1, p 1] 26 times. Cont as now set until same number of rows have been worked as on front welt. Change to size 6 needles and work in st st working patt from chart but reversing arrangement of colors. Work armhole shaping as given for front then cont on rem 84 sts until 118 rows have been worked from chart.

▦ **Shoulder and Neck Shaping**
*119th row* Cast off 10, k until there are 23 sts on right needle; leave these for right back then using correct colors, cast off 18; k to end. Cont on 33 sts now rem at end of needle for left back keeping patt correct. Cast off 10 sts at beg of next row and 6 sts at neck edge on foll row. Cast off 10 sts at beg of next row and 1 st at neck edge on

foll row. Cast off rem 6 sts to complete shoulder slope. Rejoin correct color to sts of right back, cast off 6, p to end. Cast off 10 sts at beg of next row and 1 st at neck edge on foll row. Cast off rem sts.

## RIGHT SLEEVE

▦ With size 2 needles and **2** cast on 36 sts and work in single rib for 2⅜ in (6 cm) ending with a wrong-side row. Change to size 6 needles.

▦ *Inc row* K 2, [kfb, k 1] 17 times. 53 sts. Beg with a p row work 2 rows in st st; then inc 1 st at both ends of next row; then every foll 4th row 10 times more. 75 sts. Now begin the panel in **1**.

▦ *45th row* K 74 **2**, join on **1**, k 1 **1**.

▦ *46th row* P 2 **1**, 73 **1**.

▦ *47th row* K 72 **2**, 3 **1**. Cont moving the panel in **1**, 1 st to the right-hand edge on every row for remainder of sleeve.

*At same time*, work 4 more rows without shaping then inc 1 st at both ends of next row, then every foll 8th row 3 times more. Cont on 83 sts until work measures 15⅜ in (39 cm) from beg.

▦ **Top Shaping** Cast off 1 st at beg of next 2 rows; 2 sts at beg of next 2 rows; 3 sts at beg of next 4 rows; 2 sts at beg of next 4 rows; 4 sts at beg of next 6 rows and 7 sts at beg of next 2 rows. Cast off rem 19 sts.

## LEFT SLEEVE

▦ With size 2 needles and **1** cast on 36 sts and work as given for right sleeve; cont with **1** only until work measures 13 in (33 cm) from beg then change to **3**; complete as for right sleeve using **3** only.

## MAKING UP AND NECK BORDER

▦ Join right shoulder seam. Press seams lightly on wrong side with warm iron and damp cloth. With right side facing and using size 2 needles and **2**, pick up and k 59 sts round front neck edge and 37 sts across back neck. Work in single rib for ¾ in (2 cm) then cast off loosely ribwise. Join left shoulder seam and ends of border. Sew in sleeves then join side and sleeve seams.

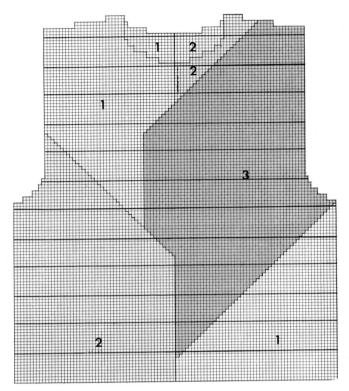

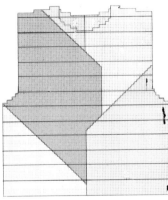

The chart above shows the arrangement of panels on the front of the three-color geometric sweater; read k rows from right to left and p rows from left to right. For the back see the smaller chart, which shows the reverse arrangement of panels; read k rows from left to right and p rows from right to left.

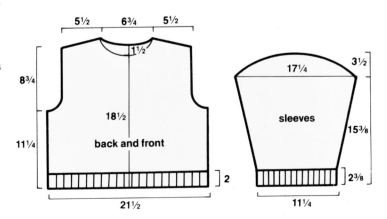

# SHE SELLS SCALLOP SHELLS

These stunning summer cotton sweaters both use reverse stocking stitch. The first has chunky cables in white and scallop shells. The second design is knitted in one piece – only the frilled edgings and the shells are knitted separately then hand sewn in place.

## SCALLOP SHELL SWEATER

### CHECKLIST

#### Materials
*Fila tricoter* Plassard, *quality Coton 6 fils: 17 balls in ecru (**E**) and 4 balls in white (**W**). Quality Coton 3 fils: 3 balls in white. Pair each of needles size 3, 4 and 6; a cable needle.*
**Note** *If the above yarn is unobtainable, refer to pages 78-9.*

#### Size
*One size, to fit bust 34/38 in; (87/97 cm). Actual measurements given on diagram.*

#### Stitches used
*Rev st st; cable patt as explained below.*

#### Tension
*Over main patt using size 6 needles, 21 sts and 26 rows to 4 in (10 cm). Work a sample on 30 sts using just one color of the main yarn and working a cable in center with 12 sts in rev st st at each side. Change needle size if necessary as explained on page 6.*
Note *Separate balls are needed for each cable and each panel of rev st st. For each cable wind off about half a ball onto a piece of cardboard.*

## INSTRUCTIONS

### BACK
▦ With size 4 needles and **E** cast on 119 sts and work in scalloped rib as foll:
▦ *1st row* (right side). K 1, * [k 1, p 1] 3 times, k 1, p 3; rep from * to last 8 sts, [k 1, p 1] 3 times, k 2.
▦ *2nd row* K 1, * [p 1, k 1] 3 times, p 1, then keeping yarn at front slip next 3 sts p-wise; rep from * to last 8 sts, [p 1, k 1] 4 times.
Rep these 2 rows 9 times more but working 3 incs evenly spaced along last row. 122 sts. Change to size 6 needles and patt; cut **E** and join on **W** at beg, then join on other colors along the row.
▦ *1st row* K 4 **W**, * p 24 **E**, k 6 **W**; rep from * twice more, p 24 **E**, k 4 **W**. The panels of **W** at each end will form cables after side incs have been worked.
▦ *2nd row* P 4 **W**, * twist yarns and take **E** to back, k 24 **E**, bring **E** to front and twist yarns, then p 6 **W**; rep from * twice more, twist yarns and take **E** to back, k 24 **E**,

bring **E** to front and twist yarns then p 4 **W**. Now begin shortened rows to form the curved shape.
▦ *3rd row* Patt 114, turn leaving 8 sts unworked at side.
▦ *4th row* Patt 106, turn leaving 8 sts unworked at this side also.
▦ *5th row* P 20 **E**, twist yarns then with **W** work the cable, slip next 3 sts on cable needle, leave at front, k 3, then k 3 from cable needle (referred to as cable 6 front), * twist yarns, p 24 **E**, twist yarns then with **W** cable 6 front; rep from * once, twist yarns, p 10 **E**, turn thus leaving 10 extra sts unworked.
▦ *6th row* Patt 86, turn. Cont to leave 10 extra sts unworked at end of next 4 rows; thus the last row was worked on center 46 sts. Cut off the last ball of **E** used and rejoin this when needed. Slip all sts onto one needle so that right side will be facing for next row.
▦ *11th row* K 4 **W**, * twist yarns, p 24 **E**, twist yarns then with **W** cable 6 front; rep from * twice more, twist yarns, p 24 **E**, twist yarns, k 4 **W**. Cont working across all sts and

cross each of the 3 cables at 6-row intervals for remainder of work. When work measures 4¾ in (12 cm) from beg, measuring along side edge, inc 1 st at both ends of next row then every foll 8th row twice more; keep these extra sts in st st using **W** and when incs are completed begin working a cable with 1 border st at each edge. Cont on these 128 sts until work measures 19¼ in (49 cm) from beg, measuring down the side, ending with a wrong-side row.
▦ **Shoulder Shaping** Cast off 30 sts at beg of next 2 rows then cont on rem 68 sts working shortened rows to shape center section. On next row patt 58 turn; on foll row patt 48, turn. Cont working 10 sts less before turning on each of next 4 rows, turn after last row and work to end. Work 1 row on wrong side across all sts but working a dec in center of each cable. Change to size 4 needles and using **E** only work in scalloped rib on rem 65 sts.
▦ *1st row* (right side). K 1, p 1, k 1, * p 3, [k 1, p 1] twice, k 1; rep from * to last 6 sts, p 3, k 1, p 1, k 1.
▦ *2nd row* K 2, p 1, * keeping yarn at front slip 3 sts p-wise, [p 1, k 1] twice, p 1; rep from * to last 6 sts, keeping yarn at front slip 3 p-wise, then p 1, k 2. Rep last 2 rows 5 times more then cast off ribwise.

### FRONT
▦ Work as for back.

### SLEEVES
▦ With size 4 needles and **E** cast on 63 sts and work in scalloped rib.
▦ *1st row* K 1, * [k 1, p 1] twice, k 1, p 3; rep from * to last 6 sts, [k 1, p 1] twice, k 2.
▦ *2nd row* K 1, * [p 1, k 1] twice, p 1, then keeping yarn at front, slip 3 p-wise; rep from * to last 6 sts, [p 1, k 1] 3 times. Rep these 2 rows 10 times more then 1st row again.
▦ *Inc row* K 3, kfb, k 3, * [pfb] 3 times, [k 3, kfb] 4 times, k 4; rep from * once, [pfb] 3 times, k 3, kfb, k 3. This row sets position for patt and must be followed exactly. Change to size 6 needles and work in patt on 82 sts.
▦ *1st row* P 8 **E**, * k 6 **W**, p 24 **E**;

rep from * once, k 6 **W**, p 8 **E**. Work 2nd row of patt as now set then begin shortened rows to form the double curve.
▦ *3rd row* Patt 38, turn leaving rem 44 sts on a spare needle. Cont on this group of sts.
▦ *4th row* Patt 34, turn.
▦ *5th row* P 4 **E**, cable 6 front using **W**, p 20 **E**, turn.
▦ *6th row* Patt 26, turn.
▦ *7th row* Patt 22, turn.
▦ *8th row* K 16 **E**, turn.
▦ *9th row* P 10 **E**, turn. K 1 row in **E** on these 10 sts then cut this ball of yarn, turn. With right side facing slip the next 18 sts of this side section onto right-hand needle, then slip the next 6 sts which are the sts of center cable and leave these 44 sts on a spare needle, now patt rem 38 sts to complete 3rd row of patt on this section.
▦ *4th row* Patt 34, turn.
▦ *5th row* P 20 **E**, cable 6 front using **W**, p 4 **E**, turn. Work from 6th row to 9th row as on first section, turn and k 1 row in **E** on these 10 sts. Now slip all the 82 sts of sleeve onto one needle so that right side will be facing.
▦ *11th row* P 8 **E**, * using **W** cable 6 front, then p 24 **E**; rep from * once, using **W** cable 6 front, p 8 **E**. Cont in patt across all sts working cables at 6-row intervals and *at same time* inc 1 st at both ends of every foll 8th row 8 times then every foll 6th row 4 times keeping extra sts at sides in rev st st using **E**. Cont on 106 sts until work measures 18½ in (47 cm) from beg. Cast off all sts.

### SHELL MOTIFS
▦ Work these before making up garment. Work first motif in first panel of rev st st on back, beg on 7th row of patt. Mark the center 10 sts of panel with right side of work facing and using size 3 needles and the thinner cotton yarn, pick up and k 10 sts along these sts by passing the needle under the horizontal thread of each st; this counts as 1st row.
▦ *2nd row* (wrong side). K 1, p 6, p 2 tog, k 1.
▦ *3rd row* [K 2, p 1] twice, k 2 tog, k 1.
▦ *4th row* K 1, p 1, kfb, p 2, kfb, p 1, k 1.

*cool summer sweaters*

*5th row* K 2, pfb, p 1, k 2, p 1, pfb, k 2.

*6th row* K 1, p 1, kfb, k 2, p 2, k 2, kfb, p 1, k 1.

*7th row* K 2, pfb, p 3, k 2, p 3, pfb, k 2.

*8th row* K 1, p 1, kfb, k 4, p 2, k 4, kfb, p 1, k 1.

*9th row* K 2, pfb, p 1, k 2, pfb, p 1, k 2 (the center 2 sts), p 1, pfb, k 2, p 1, pfb, k 2. 22 sts.

*10th row* K 1, p 1, [k 3, p 2] 3 times, k 3, p 1, k 1.

*11th row* [K 2, p 3] 4 times, k 2.

*12th row* As 10th.

*13th row* [K 2, pfb, p 2] twice, [k 2, p 2, pfb] twice, k 2. 26 sts.

*14th row* K 1, p 1, [k 4, p 2] 3 times, k 4, p 1, k 1.

*15th row* [K 2, p 4] 4 times, k 2.

*16th row* As 14th.

Keeping patt correct as now set cast off 3 sts at beg of next 3 rows and 4 sts at beg of next 2 rows. Cast off rem 6 sts. Slip-st shell motif in place so that it covers a total of 14 rows at center. Skip

next 10 rows then work another motif; work 2 more motifs in same panel leaving 10 rows between them. Work motifs in same way in each of the rem 3 panels of rev st st on back. Work similar motifs on front. Work motifs in same way on sleeves on the 2 complete panels of rev st st but do not work any on the side panels.

## MAKING UP

Join shoulder seams and sides of neck border backstitching these and all seams. Press all seams lightly on wrong side with warm iron and damp cloth using point of iron on ribbed sections. Pin cast-off edge of sleeves to sides of sweater placing center of sleeves level with shoulder seams and sides of sleeves approx 9¾ in (25 cm) down from shoulders; ensure that sides of sleeves are at same level on patt at each side. Sew in place as pinned then join side and sleeve seams.

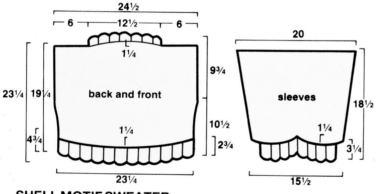

**SHELL MOTIF SWEATER**

## Materials

*Phildar* Florenlin: 15 (16) balls No 3 (salmon). *Pair each of needles size 3 and 4; a circular needle size 4 in order to accommodate all sts for the full width of sweater.*
**Note** *If the above yarn is unobtainable, refer to pages 78-9.*

## Sizes

*Two sizes, to fit bust 32/34 (36/38) in; 82/87 (92/97) cm. Actual measurements shown on diagram.*

## Stitches used

*Rev st st; g st; st st; m st.*

## Tension

*Over rev st st using size 4 needles, 21 sts and 30 rows to 4 in (10 cm). Work a sample on 27 sts and change needle size if necessary as explained on page 6.*

## INSTRUCTIONS

### BACK

With pair of size 4 needles cast on 97 (105) sts for lower edge of front; frilled edging is worked later. Beg with a p row work in rev st st but inc 1 st at both ends of every foll 6th row 10 (11) times then every foll 4th row 3 (2) times. Cont on 123 (131) sts until work measures 10¼ (10⅝) in, 26 (27) cm, from beg. End with k row.

**Sleeve Shaping** Cast on 3 sts at beg of next 4 rows, 5 sts at beg of next 20 (16) rows and 6 sts at beg of next 12 (16) rows; change to circular needle during these rows for ease of working and cont working backwards and forwards in rows as usual. Cont on 307 (319) sts until work measures 4⅜ (4¾) in, 11 (12) cm, along outer edge measured after last casting-on, ending with a k row.

**Neck Shaping** *1st row* P 140 (146) and leave these sts of left front on circular needle, then using a straight needle, cast off next 27 sts, p to end. Cont on 140 (146) sts now rem on needle for right front and work 1 row straight. ** Cast off 4 sts at beg of next row and foll alt row, 2 sts at same edge on next alt row and 1 st on foll alt row. 129 (135) sts. ** Place a marker loop of contrast yarn at side edge to mark shoulder line and cont for right back. K 1 row then for back neck shaping cast on 6 sts at beg of next row and next alt row. K 1 row thus ending at neck edge then cut yarn and leave these 141 (147) sts on a spare needle. With wrong side facing rejoin yarn to neck edge of left front sts and work as for right front from ** to **. P 1 row without shaping thus reaching the shoulder line; place marker loop at side edge then cont for left back. Work 2 rows straight then for back neck cast on 6 sts at beg of next row and next alt row.

*Next row* Using the circular needle p 141 (147) sts of left back, turn, cast on 25 sts, turn, then p 141 (147) sts of right back. 307 (319) sts. Cont across all sts until work measures 5½ (5⅞) in, 14 (15) cm from shoulder markers ending with a k row.

**Sleeve Shaping** Cast off 6 sts at beg of next 12 (16) rows, 5 sts at beg of next 20 (16) rows and 3 sts at beg of next 4 rows. Cont on rem 123 (131) sts using pair of needles; work 6 (7) rows without shaping then dec 1 st at both ends of next row, then every foll 4th row twice (once), work 3 rows straight then dec 1 st at both ends of next row, then every foll 6th row 9 (10) times. Cont on rem 97 (105) sts until work measures 10¼ (10⅝) in, 26 (27) cm, from the last casting-off at end of sleeve shaping measured on the straight. Cast off.

### LOWER BORDERS

With size 3 needles cast on 169 (183) sts for outer edge of border.

*1st row* P 2, * k 11, p 3; rep from * to last 13 sts, k 11, p 2.

*2nd row* K 2, * p 11, k 3; rep from * to last 13 sts, p 11, k 2.

*3rd row* P 2, * k 3, k 2 tog, k 1, SKPO, k 3, p 3; rep from * to last 13 sts, k 3, k 2 tog, k 1, SKPO, k 3, p 2.

*4th row* K 2, * p 9, k 3; rep from * to last 11 sts, p 9, k 2.

*5th row* P 2, * k 9, p 3; rep from * to last 11 sts, k 9, p 2.

*6th row* As 4th.

*7th row* P 2, * k 2, k 2 tog, k 1, SKPO, k 2, p 3; rep from * to last 11 sts, k 2, k 2 tog, k 1, SKPO, k 2, p 2.

*8th row* K 2, * p 7, k 3; rep from * to last 9 sts, p 7, k 2.

*9th row* P 2, * k 7, p 3; rep from * to last 9 sts, k 7, p 2.

*10th row* As 8th.

*11th row* P 2, * k 1, k 2 tog, k 1, SKPO, k 1, p 3; rep from * to last 9 sts, k 1, k 2 tog, k 1, SKPO, k 1, p 2.

*12th row* K 2, * p 5, k 3; rep from * to last 7 sts, p 5, k 2.

*13th row* P 2, * k 5, p 3; rep from * to last 7 sts, k 5, p 2. Rep last 2 rows once. Cast off rem 97 (105) sts. Work another border in same way.

### SLEEVE BORDERS

With size 3 needles cast on 113 (127) sts and work as for lower border; when the 15th row has been worked cast off rem 65 (73) sts. Work another border in same way.

## COLLAR

With size 3 needles cast on 265 sts for upper edge of collar.

*1st row* (right side). K 1, * k 11, p 3; rep from * to last 12 sts, k 12.

*2nd row* K 1, * p 11, k 3; rep from * to last 12 sts, p 11, k 1. The patt is thus arranged in same way as on lower border but with 1 st in g st at each side instead of p 2 rib.

*3rd row* K 1, * k 3, k 2 tog, k 1, SKPO, k 3, p 3; rep from * to last 12 sts, k 3, k 2 tog, k 1, SKPO, k 4. Cont to dec on the st st panels in same way as on lower border on 7th and 11th rows, always keeping the edge st in g st at each side. Work 1 row on rem 151 sts then shape for neck edge.

*13th row* (right side). Cast off 34, patt to end.

*14th row* Cast off 56, patt to end. Cast off 4 sts at beg of next 6 rows then cast off rem 37 sts.

## SCALLOP SHELL

Beg at lower edge cast on 59 sts using size 3 needles.

*1st row* (right side). K 1, * k 7, p 3; rep from * to last 8 sts, k 8.

*2nd row* K 1, * p 7, k 3; rep from * to last 8 sts, p 7, k 1. Rep these 2 rows 4 times more.

*11th row* K 1, * k 1, k 2 tog, k 1, SKPO, k 1, p 2 tog, p 1; rep from * to last 8 sts, k 1, k 2 tog, k 1, SKPO, k 2. 42 sts.

*12th row* K 1, * p 5, k 2; rep from * to last 6 sts, p 5, k 1.

*13th row* K 1, * k 5, p 2; rep from * to last 6 sts, k 6. Rep last 2 rows 3 times more, then 12th row again.

*21st row* K 1, * k 2 tog, k 1, SKPO, p 2 tog; rep from * to last 6 sts, k 2 tog, k 1, SKPO, k 1. 25 sts.

*22nd row* K 1, * p 3, k 1; rep from * to end.

*23rd row* K 1, * k 3, p 1; rep from * to last 4 sts, k 4. Rep last 2 rows 3 times more, then 22nd row again. Cast off.

For upper section cast on 42 sts.

*1st row* As 13th row of upper section.

*2nd row* As 12th row of upper section. Rep these 2 rows once.

*5th row* K 1, * k 2 tog, k 1, SKPO, p 2; rep from * to last 6 sts, k 2 tog, k 1, SKPO, k 1. 30 sts.

*6th row* K 1, * p 3, k 2; rep from * to last 4 sts, p 3, k 1.

*7th row* K 1, * k 3, p 2; rep from * to last 4 sts, k 4.

*8th row* K 1, * p 3, k 2 tog; rep from * to last 4 sts, p 3, k 1. Rep 23rd and 22nd rows of main part of motif then cast off.

## COCKLE SHELLS

With size 3 needles cast on 3 sts and p these sts; now work in st st and shape as folls:

*1st row* K 1, kfb, k 1.

*2nd row* P 4.

*3rd row* K 1, [kfb] twice, k 1.

*4th row* P 6.

*5th row* K 1, [kfb] 4 times, k 1.

*6th row* P 10.

*7th row* K 2, [kfb, k 1] twice, kfb, k 3. Cont on these 13 sts and work 3 rows in st st then cont in g st and work 2 rows without shaping.

*13th row* K 3, [kfb, k 2] 3 times, k 1. Work 3 rows in g st on these 16 sts.

*17th row* [K 2, kfb] 5 times, k 1. Cont on these 21 sts and work 7 rows in g st. Cast off. Make 5 more shells in same way.

## WINKLE SHELLS

Each shell consists of 3 triangles of different length. For 1st triangle cast on 12 sts and work in st st; k 1 row then dec 1 st at *end* of next row, then at same edge on every alt row until 3 sts rem. Cast off. For 2nd triangle cast on 10 sts and work in same way. For 3rd triangle cast on 8 sts and work in same way. Join the 3 triangles to form the shape as shown in photo. Make 6 more shells in same way.

## SEAWEED

For one strip cast on 3 sts using size 3 needles. Work in moss st.

*1st row* (count this as right side for 1st strip). K 1, p 1, k 1. *2nd row* As 1st. Keeping m st correct cont working from chart working incs at beg of wrong-side rows where shown and casting off 7 sts at beg of 48th, 68th and 88th rows and 5 sts at beg of 104th row. Complete as shown on chart. Work second strip in same way but counting 1st row as wrong side thus reversing the shape.

## MAKING UP

With right sides tog sew cast-off edge of one lower border to lower edge of front easing in front slightly to fit. Sew other border to lower edge of back. Sew cast-off edge of sleeve borders to outer edges of sleeves. Pin cast-off edge of collar to neck edges as folls: first mark center of front neck. The edge where the first group of sts was cast off should be placed 4 sts beyond the center towards the right front; pin cast-on edge around neck towards the left shoulder, then around back neck and right front and the remainder of border overlaps first section to end close to left front shoulder edge. Sew in place as pinned.

Now sew on the motifs, padding each motif slightly with a few oddments of the yarn. Backstitch cast-off edges of upper and lower sections of scallop shell tog drawing in the seam slightly. Slip-st shell to center front with upper edge about 1 ½ in (4 cm) below neckline. Slip-st a winkle shell to center front below the scallop as shown, then on either side of this alternate a cockle shell and a winkle shell in a curved line up to each shoulder. Sew the seaweed on each side of neck as shown. Lastly join side and sleeve seams with backstitch.

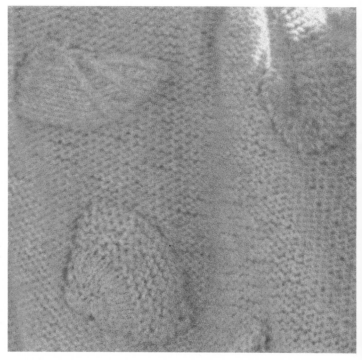

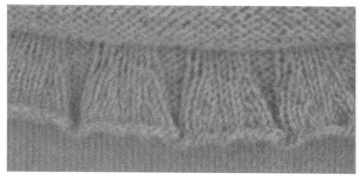

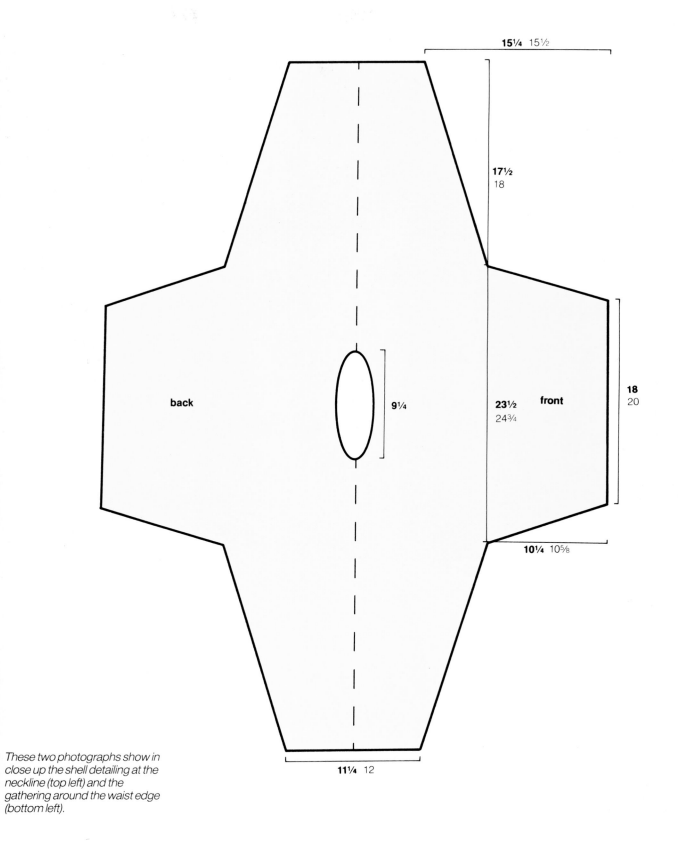

**15¼** 15½

**17½**
18

**9¼**

back

**23½**
24¾

front

**18**
20

**10¼** 10⅝

**11¼** 12

*These two photographs show in close up the shell detailing at the neckline (top left) and the gathering around the waist edge (bottom left).*

# GIANT JUMPER

## CHECKLIST

### Materials
*Novita Fauna, 1,350 g. Pair of needles size 9; set of double-pointed needles in same size for neck border.*
**Note** *If the above yarn is unobtainable, refer to pages 78-9.*

### Size
*One size, to fit bust 32/38 in (82/87) cm. Actual measurements shown on diagram.*

### Stitches used
St st; g st; patt No 1; block patt, *worked over a multiple of 10 sts plus 2 as folls:*

> 1st row *(right side). K 1, * k 5, p 5;* rep from* to* ending k 1.*
> 2nd row *(wrong side). As 1st. Rep these 2 rows once.*
> 5th row *K 1, * p 5, k 5;* rep from* to* ending k 1.*
> 6th to 8th rows *As 5th. These 8 rows form one patt.*

Patt No 2; diagonal rib patt, *worked over a multiple of 4 sts plus 2 as folls:*

> 1st row *(right side). * K 2, p 2;* rep from* to* ending k 2.*
> 2nd row *\* P 2, k 2;* rep from* to* ending p 2.*
> 3rd row *K 1, * p 2, k 2;* rep from* to* ending p 1.*
> 4th row *As 3rd.*
> 5th row *\* P 2, k 2;* rep from* to* ending p 2.*
> 6th row *\* K 2, p 2;* rep from* to* ending k 2.*
> 7th row *P 1, * k 2, p 2;* rep from* to* ending k 1.*
> 8th row *As 7th. These 8 rows form one patt.*

Patt No 3; waffle patt, *worked over a multiple of 3 sts plus 1 as folls:*
> 1st row *(right side). P 1, * k 2, p 1;* rep from* to*.*
> 2nd row *K 1, * p 2, k 1;* rep from* to*.*
> 3rd row *As 1st.*
> 4th row *K all sts. These 4 rows form one patt.*

Patt No 4; mitre patt, *worked on an even number of sts as folls:*
> 1st row *(right side). K.*
> 2nd row. *P.*
> 3rd row *K 1, * k 2 tog; rep from* to last st, k 1.*
> 4th row *K 1, * k 1 then pick up loop lying between st just worked and next st and k this loop without twisting it;* rep from* to* ending k 1. This restores correct number of sts. These 4 rows form one patt.*

### Tensions
*All with size 9 needles and double yarn; over patts No 1 and 2, 13 sts and 20 rows to 4 in (10 cm). Patt No 3 gives a slightly tighter tension in width but the same length tension. Over patt No 4, 13 sts and 21 rows to 4 in (10 cm).*
Note *Yarn is used double throughout; take 2 balls and wind them tog to form a double thickness ball which is easier to use.*

## INSTRUCTIONS

### BACK
▦ Cast on 82 sts and work 4 rows in st st beg with a k row. Now work 20 rows in patt No 1, then 2 rows in g st, then 22 rows in patt No 2, then 2 rows in g st, then 20 rows in patt No 3, then 2 rows in g st, then 28 rows in patt No 4, then 2 rows in g st, then 32 rows in patt No 1.
▦ **Shoulder Shaping** *Next row*
Cast off 20, k until there are 42 sts on right needle, leave these on a holder for neck border, cast off rem 20 sts and fasten off.

### FRONT
▦ Work exactly as for back.

### SLEEVES
▦ Cast on 52 sts and work 4 rows in st st. Now work in patt No 1 but inc 1 st at both ends of 8th row of 1st and 2nd patts; work 4 more rows in patt then work 2 rows in g st and inc at both ends of 2nd of these rows. 58 sts.
▦ Now work in patt No 2 but inc 1 st at both ends of 8th row of 1st and 2nd patts; work 6 more rows in patt then work 2 rows in g st and inc at both ends of 2nd of these rows. 64 sts.
▦ Now work in patt No 3 but inc 1 at both ends of every foll 6th row 3 times then work 2 more rows in patt; 20 rows have been worked in this patt. Work 2 rows in g st without shaping. 70 sts.
▦ Now work in patt No 4; inc 1 st at both ends of 2nd row of 1st patt then cont on 72 sts without shaping. Work 24 more rows ending with 2nd patt row. Work 2 rows in g st then cast off all sts.

## MAKING UP AND NECK BORDER
▦ Join shoulder seams. With right side of work facing and using double-pointed needles, k the sts from holder at front neck then k those of back neck. Join into a ring and work in rounds of st st for 5 rounds then cast off loosely.
▦ Pin cast-off edge of sleeves to sides of sweater placing center of sleeve level with shoulder seam and ensuring that sides of sleeves reach to same position on patt at each side. Sew in place as pinned then join side and sleeve seams matching patts and bands of g st. The st st borders at lower edges and at neck will roll slightly onto right side.

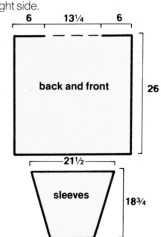

Diagram:
- back and front: 6, 13¼, 6 (top), 21½ (bottom), 26 (height)
- sleeves: 16 (bottom), 18¾ (height)

# Aran knitting for a lounger

# ARAN BEAUTY

The softest, subtlest greens of an Irish landscape are chosen for this original variation on an Aran sweater. Cotton yarns in two shades are knitted together to reflect the variety of nature. The sweater opens at the back, with a V-shaped neck and three big buttons. Picot edgings are worked on the ribs for a delicate finishing touch.

## CHECKLIST

### Materials
*Pingouin Fil d'Ecosse No 5: 8 balls céleste ondine No 48 and 8 balls buvard No 33. Pair each of needles size 4, 5 and 6; a cable needle; an extra pair of needles size 5 for neck border; 3 buttons.*

### Size
*One size, to fit bust 34/38 in (87/97 cm). Actual measurements shown on diagram.*

### Stitches used
Single rib; rev st st; cable 6 back (or front) = *slip next 3 sts on cable needle, leave at back (or front), k 3, then k 3 from cable needle;* C 4 R = *cross 4 right thus, slip next st on cable needle, leave at back, k 3, then p 1 from cable needle;* C 4 L = *cross 4 left thus, slip next 3 sts on cable needle, leave at front, p 1, then k 3 from cable needle;* C 3 R = *cross 3 right thus, slip next st on cable needle, leave at back, k 2, then p 1 from cable needle;* C 3 L = *cross 3 left thus, slip next 2 sts on cable needle, leave at front, p 1, then k 2 from cable needle;* MB = *make bobble thus, into next st p into front then [k into back then into front of same st] twice;* CB = *complete bobble thus, with yarn at back slip the 5 sts onto right needle, yarn over needle and pass the 5 sts one at a time over the made loop;* T 2 = *twist 2 thus, pass needle in front of 1st st, lift up 2nd st and k it, leaving it on needle, then k 1st st and slip both off needle.*
*The various panels of patt are worked as folls:*
Twist rib, *worked over 2 sts.*
   1st row *T 2.*
   2nd row *P 2. Rep these 2 rows throughout.*
Chain cable *worked over 14 sts as folls:*
   1st row *P 4, k 6, p 4.*
   2nd row *K 4, p 6, k 4.*
   3rd row *P 4, cable 6 back, p 4.*
   4th row *As 2nd.*
   5th to 8th rows *Rep 1st and 2nd rows twice more.*
   9th row *As 3rd.*
   10th row *As 2nd.*
   11th row *P 3, C 4 R, C 4 L, p 3.*
   12th row *K 3, p 3, k 2, p 3, k 3.*
   13th row *P 3, k 3, p 2, k 3, p 3.*
   14th to 24th rows *Rep 12th and 13th rows 5 times more, then 12th row again.*
   25th row *P 3, C 4 L, C 4 R, p 3.*
   26th row *As 2nd. These last 24 rows from 3rd to 26th inclusive, form one patt.*
Lobster Claw, *worked over 9 sts as folls:*
   1st row *K 9.*
   2nd row *P 9.*
   3rd row *Slip 3 sts on cable needle, leave at back, k 1, then k 3 from cable needle, k next st, now slip foll st on cable needle, leave at front, k 3, then k 1 from cable needle.*
   4th row *P 9. These 4 rows form one patt.*

Zig-zag panel 1 *(moving to the left first). Worked over 14 sts as folls:*
   1st row *P 3, k 2, p 9.*
   2nd row *K 9, p 2, k 3.*
   3rd row *P 3, C 3 L, p 8.*
   4th row *K 8, p 2, k 4.*
   5th row *P 4, C 3 L, p 7.*
   6th row *K 7, p 2, k 5.*
   7th row *P 5, C 3 L, p 6.*
   8th row *K 6, p 2, k 6.*
   9th row *P 6, C 3 L, p 5.*
   10th row *K 5, p 2, k 7.*
   11th row *P 7, C 3 L, p 4.*
   12th row *K 4, p 2, k 8.*
   13th row *P 5, MB, p 2, C 3 L, p 3.*
   14th row *K 3, p 2, k 3, p 5, k 5.*
   15th row *P 5, CB, p 2, C 3 R, p 3.*
   16th row *As 12th.*
   17th row *P 7, C 3 R, p 4.*
   18th row *As 10th.*
   19th row *P 6, C 3 R, p 5.*
   20th row *As 8th.*
   21st row *P 5, C 3 R, p 6.*
   22nd row *As 6th.*
   23rd row *P 4, C 3 R, p 7.*
   24th row *As 4th.*
   25th row *P 3, C 3 R, p 2, MB, p 5.*
   26th row *K 5, p 5, k 3, p 2, k 3.*
   27th row *P 3, C 3 L, p 2, CB, p 5.*
   28th row *As 4th.*
*These last 24 rows from 5th to 28th inclusive, form one patt for this panel.*
Zig-zag panel 2 *(moving to the right first). Worked over 14 sts as folls:*
   1st row *P 9, k 2, p 3.*
   2nd row *K 3, p 2, k 9.*
   3rd row *P 8, C 3 R, p 3.*
   4th row *K 4, p 2, k 8.*
   5th to 16th rows *Rep from 17th row to 28th row of zig-zag panel 1.*
   17th to 28th rows *Rep from 5th row to 16th row of zig-zag panel 1.*
*These last 24 rows from 5th to 28th inclusive, form one patt. Note that the sts of each panel must always be counted as 14 sts. Do not make a bobble in a place where you will shortly be working a dec.*
Plaited cable, *worked over 24 sts as folls:*
   1st row *K 24.*
   2nd row *P 24.*
   3rd row *[Cable 6 back] 4 times.*
   4th row *P 24.*
   5th and 6th rows *As 1st and 2nd.*
   7th row *K 3, [cable 6 front] 3 times, k 3.*
   8th row *P 24. These 8 rows form one patt.*
Single cable, *worked over 6 sts as folls:*
   1st row *K 6.*
   2nd row *P 6.*
   3rd and 4th rows *As 1st and 2nd.*
   5th row *Cable 6 back.*
   6th row *P 6. These 6 rows form one patt.*

### Tensions
Over rev st st using size 6 needles and the yarn double, 22 sts and 27 rows to 4 in (10 cm). Overall tension measured over a combination of patts, 24 sts and 27 rows to 4 in (10 cm).

*soft sweater in Irish stitches*

## INSTRUCTIONS

Throughout work use a strand of each color tog.

### FRONT

▦ With size 4 needles cast on 90 sts. ✲✲ Beg with a p row work 2 rows in st st.

▦ *Next row* P 1, ✲ yrn, p 2 tog; rep from ✲ to last st, p 1. Work 2 more rows in st st. ✲✲ This completes picot edging; (after a few more rows have been worked fold up the cast-on edge to wrong side, folding along center of line of holes and slip-st in place on wrong side so that measurements can be taken from lower edge.) Change to size 5 needles and work in rib.

▦ *1st row* (right side). K 2, ✲ p 2, k 2; rep from ✲ to end.

▦ *2nd row* P 2, ✲ k 2, p 2; rep from ✲ to end. Rep these 2 rows until work measures 2¾ in (7 cm) from lower edge, ending with a 1st rib row.

▦ *Inc row* ✲ K 4, p 2, [kfb] twice, p 6, [kfb] twice, p 2, kfb, k 1, [pfb, p 1] 3 times, kfb, k 1, p 2, [kfb, k 1] 3 times, ✲ p 1, [pfb, p 2] 5 times, pfb, p 1, [kfb, k 1] 3 times, p 2, kfb, k 1, [pfb, p 1] 3 times, kfb, k 1, p 2, [kfb] twice, p 6, [kfb] twice, p 2, k 4. This row sets positions for patt and must be followed very carefully.

Change to size 6 needles and work in patt on 120 sts as folls:

▦ *1st row* P 4, T 2, work 1st row of chain cable, T 2, p 3, work 1st row of lobster claw, work 1st row of zig-zag panel 1, work 1st row of plaited cable, work 1st row of zig-zag panel 2, work 1st row of lobster claw, p 3, T 2, work 1st row of chain cable, T 2, p 4. Cont in patt as now set for 3 more rows then inc 1 st at both ends of next row, then every foll 6th row 9 times more keeping extra sts at sides in rev st st. Cont on 140 sts until work measures 12⅝ in (32 cm) from lower edge; place marker loops of contrast yarn at each end to indicate beg of armholes. Cont without shaping until work measures 17⅜ in (44 cm) from lower edge, ending with a wrong-side row.

▦ **Neck Shaping** *Next row* Patt 56 and leave these sts of left front on a spare needle, cast off next 28 sts, patt to end. Cont on 56 sts now rem on needle for right front and work 1 row straight. ✲✲✲ Cast off 3 sts at beg of next row and foll alt row, 2 sts at same edge on next 4 alt rows and 1 st on foll 5 alt rows. Cont on rem 37 sts until work measures 21¼ in (54 cm) from lower edge. Cast off all sts for shoulder edge.

▦ Rejoin yarns to neck edge of left front sts and complete as for right front from ✲✲✲ to end.

### LEFT BACK

▦ With size 4 needles cast on 48 sts and work as for front from ✲✲ to ✲✲; complete picot edging later, as on front.

▦ Change to size 5 needles and rib.

▦ *1st row* ✲ P 2, k 2; rep from ✲ to end. Rep this row until same number of rows have been worked as on front thus ending with a right-side row.

▦ *Inc row* Rep from ✲ to ✲ in the inc row of front, p 6, kfb, k 1, p 2, k 2. 61 sts. Change to size 6 needles and patt.

▦ *1st row* P 2, T 2, p 3, work 1st row of single cable, work 1st row of zig-zag No 2, work 1st row of lobster claw, p 3, T 2, work 1st row of chain cable, T 2, p 4. Cont in patt as now set for 3 more rows then to shape side, inc 1 st at *end* of next row, then at same edge on every foll 6th row 9 times more, keeping extra sts at side in rev st st.

Cont on 71 sts until work measures 12⅝ in (32 cm) from lower edge; place marker loop at side edge to indicate beg of armhole. Cont without shaping until work measures 13⅜ in (34 cm) from lower edge, ending at the straight center back edge.

▦ **Neck Shaping** Dec 1 st at beg of next row, then at same edge on next 2 rows, then work 1 row straight; rep last 4 rows 8 times more. Now dec 1 st at same edge on next 7 alt rows then cont on rem 37 sts until work matches front to shoulder edge. Cast off all sts.

### RIGHT BACK

▦ Work as for left back but reversing the double rib, the inc row and arrangement of patt, also reverse all shapings.

### SLEEVES

▦ With size 4 needles cast on 54 sts and work from ✲✲ to ✲✲ as on front; complete picot edging later. Change to size 5 needles and work in double rib as on front but beg with 2nd row which will be right side. Cont until work measures 2¾ in (7 cm) from lower edge, ending with a 2nd row.

▦ *Inc row* P 6, [kfb] twice, p 2, kfb, k 1, [pfb, p 1] 3 times, kfb, k 1, [pfb twice, p 1] 4 times, [pfb] twice, kfb, k 1, [pfb, p 1] 3 times, kfb, k 1, p 2, [kfb] twice, p 6. 78 sts. Change to size 6 needles and patt.

▦ *1st row* Working the last 10 sts of chain cable, k 6, p 4, then T 2, p 3, work 1st row of lobster

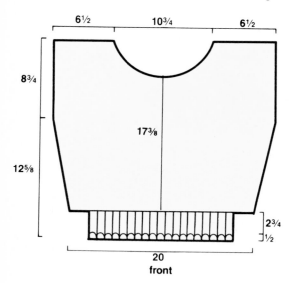

6½  10¾  6½

8¾

17⅜

12⅝

2¾

½

20

**front**

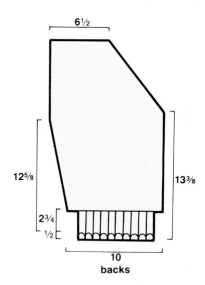

6½

12⅝

13⅜

2¾

½

10

**backs**

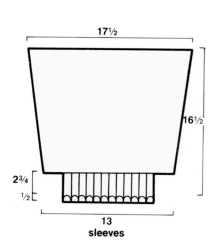

17½

16½

2¾

½

13

**sleeves**

claw, p 3, work 1st row of plaited cable, p 3, work 1st row of lobster claw, p 3, T 2, then working first 10 sts of chain cable, p 4, k 6. Cont in patt as now set for 5 rows then inc 1 st at both ends of next row, then every foll 8th row 4 times, then every foll 6th row 8 times. The first 4 sts added each side will complete the chain cable, then the next 2 sts form a twist rib and the rem 7 sts should be worked in rev st st. Cont on 104 sts until work measures 16½ in (42 cm) from lower edge. Cast off all sts.

## MAKING UP AND BORDERS

▦ Join shoulder seams matching patt. With right side of work facing and using 3 of the size 5 needles, pick up and k 81 sts along straight center back edge of left back, 42 sts along sloping edge, 76 sts around front neck edge, 42 sts along sloping edge on right back and 81 sts along straight center back edge. Using the 4th needle work in rows of double rib as on front welt but beg with 2nd row.

After 4 rows have been worked make buttonholes.

▦ *Next row* Beg at lower edge of right back, wrong side facing, rib 18, cast off 4, [rib until there are 24 sts on right needle after previous buttonhole, cast off 4] twice, rib to end. On foll row cast on 4 sts over each buttonhole. Work 4 more rows in rib then cast off ribwise.

▦ With right side of work facing and using size 4 needles, pick up and k 42 sts along cast-off edge of ribbed border on left back neck, 76 sts along edge of front neck border and 42 sts along corresponding edge on right back. Rep from ** to ** as on front. Cast off. Fold this cast-off edge to wrong side along center of line of holes and slip-st in place. Sew cast-off edge of sleeves to sides of armholes between markers. Join side and sleeve seams. Sew buttons to right back to correspond with buttonholes.

*1 Plaited Cable*

*2 Lobster Claw*

*3 Twist Rib*

*4 Zig Zag Panel*

*5 Chain Cable*

*6 Single Cable*

# LACY COTTON TOPS

Three simple tops are given a little luxury with satin ribbon woven through the lacy knitting. The center and far right designs are based on the same slanted lace pattern. For the top on the right, the ribbon is threaded only on one diagonal, for the design in the middle, the ribbons are knotted where they cross, and the simpler knit on the left has vertical patterns.

## CHECKLIST

### Materials

*Pingouin* Coton Naturel 4 fils: *for each top, 3 (3) balls in white. Pair each of needles size 0 and 2; approx 16½ yd (15 metres) of narrow ribbon.*

### Sizes

*Two sizes, to fit bust 32 (34/36) in; 82 (87/92) cm. Actual measurements shown on diagram.*

### Stitches used

Single rib; zig-zag lace patt, *used for No 1 and No 2, worked on a multiple of 24 sts plus 10 as folls:*

1st row *(right side).* K 4, * yfd, SKPO, k 6; rep from * to last 6 sts, yfd, SKPO, k 4.

2nd and alt rows P.

3rd row K 3, * yfd, SKPO, yfd, k 2 tog, k 4; rep from * to last 7 sts, yfd, SKPO, yfd, k 2 tog, k 3.

5th row K 2, * yfd, SKPO, k 2, yfd, k 2 tog, k 2; rep from * to end.

7th row K 7, * yfd, k 2 tog, k 6; rep from * to last 3 sts, yfd, k 2 tog, k 1.

9th row K 8, * yfd, k 2 tog, k 6; rep from * to last 2 sts, k 2.

11th row K 1, * yfd, k 2 tog, k 4, yfd, SKPO, k 6, yfd, SKPO, yfd, k 2 tog, k 4, yfd, SKPO; rep from * to last 1 (9) sts, then for 1st size k 1, (for 2nd size yfd, k 2 tog, k 4, yfd, SKPO, k 1).

13th row K 1, * yfd, k 2 tog, k 3, yfd, SKPO, k 6, yfd, SKPO, k 2, yfd, k 2 tog, k 2, yfd, SKPO, k 1; rep from * to last 1 (9) sts, then for 1st size k 1, (for 2nd size yfd, k 2 tog, k 3, yfd, SKPO, k 2).

15th row K 5, * yfd, SKPO, k 6; rep from * to last 5 sts, yfd, SKPO, k 3.

16th row P. These 16 rows form one patt.

Vertical lace patt, *used for No 3 worked on a multiple of 8 sts plus 1 as folls:*

1st row *(right side).* K 3, * k 2 tog, yfd, k 6; rep from * to last 6 sts, k 2 tog, yfd, k 4.

2nd row P 3, * p 2 tog, yrn, p 6; rep from * to last 6 sts, p 2 tog, yrn, p 4. These 2 rows form one patt.

## Tensions

*For either patt using size 2 needles, 26 sts and 36 rows to 4 in (10 cm). For the zigzag patt work a sample on 34 sts working as for 2nd size on 11th and 13th rows. For the vertical lace patt work a sample on 33 sts.*

## INSTRUCTIONS

### STYLE 1
### BACK

▦ With size 0 needles cast on 117 sts (125) sts and work in single rib.

▦ 1st row (right side). P 1, * k 1, p 1; rep from * to end.

▦ 2nd row K 1, * p 1, k 1; rep from * to end. Rep these 2 rows until work measures 2⅜ in (6 cm) from beg, ending with a 1st rib row. ** Change to size 2 needles and p 1 row on wrong side working 5 incs evenly spaced. 122 (130) sts. Now work in zig-zag lace patt as given

*ribbon-work finery*

above; cont until work measures 12⅝ (13⅜) in, 32 (34) cm, from beg, ending with a p row.

▨ **Armhole Shaping** Cast off 4 sts at beg of next 6 rows. Cont on rem 98 (106) sts keeping patt correct as far as possible; any sts at sides which cannot be fitted into patt should be worked in st st. Cont until work measures 15¾ (17) in, 40 (43) cm from beg, ending with a p row.

▨ **Neck Shaping** *Next row* Patt 43 (45) sts and leave these on a spare needle for one side of neck, cast off next 12 (16) sts, patt to end. Cont on 43 (45) sts now rem on needle and work 1 row straight. *** Cast off 4 sts at beg of next row and foll alt row, 3 sts at same edge on next 2 alt rows, 2 sts on next 2 alt rows and 1 st on foll 9 alt rows. Cont on rem 16 (18) sts until work measures 20½ (21⅝) in, 52 (55) cm from beg. Cast off these sts for shoulder edge. *** With wrong side facing rejoin yarn to neck edge of other group of sts and complete as for first side of neck from *** to ***.

## FRONT
▨ Work exactly as for back.

## BORDERS
▨ All worked with size 0 needles; they are knitted separately and sewn on for extra firmness. For armhole border cast on 151 (157) sts and work in rib as on welt for 10 rows. Cast off loosely ribwise. Work another border in same way. For back neck border cast on 121 (125) sts and work as for armhole border; work another border in same way for front neck.

## MAKING UP
▨ Sew cast-on edge of neck borders to neck edges. Join entire shoulder seams. Sew cast-on edge of armhole borders to armhole edges. Join side seams and ends of borders. Press seams lightly on wrong side with warm iron and damp cloth avoiding ribbing.

▨ Beg at bottom right-hand corner of back, thread ribbon through holes as shown in sketch No 1; trim front in same way.

## STYLE 2
Work exactly as for No 1 but thread the ribbons through as shown in sketch No 2 forming knots where the ribbons cross each other.

## STYLE 3
### BACK
▨ Work as given for No 1 as far as *** then change to size 2 needles and p 1 row on wrong side working 4 incs evenly spaced. 121 (129) sts. Now work in vertical lace patt and cont without shaping until work measures 12⅝ (13⅜) in, 32 (34 cm) from beg, ending with a 2nd patt row.

▨ **Armhole Shaping** Cast off 4 sts at beg of next 6 rows. 97 (105) sts. The 1st patt row will now begin k 7 and end k 8; 2nd patt row will begin p 7 and end p 8. Cont without shaping until work measures 15¾ (17) in, 40 (43) cm from beg, ending with a 2nd patt row.

▨ **Neck Shaping** *1st row* Patt 43 (45) and leave these sts on a spare needle for one side of neck, cast off next 11 (15) sts, patt to end. Cont on 43 (45) sts now rem on needle and work 1 row straight. Complete as for No 1 from *** to ***. Rejoin yarn to neck edge of other group of sts and complete as for No 1 from *** to ***

### FRONT
▨ Work exactly as for back.

### BORDERS
▨ Work these as for No 1.

### MAKING UP
▨ As for No 1; thread the ribbon through vertical lines; on one line pass alternately over 2 threads and under 2 threads and for the next line pass under 2 threads then over 8 threads.

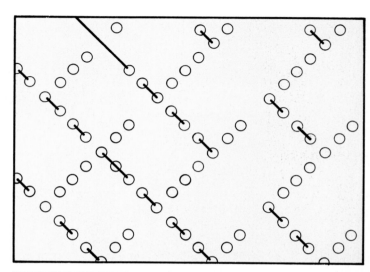

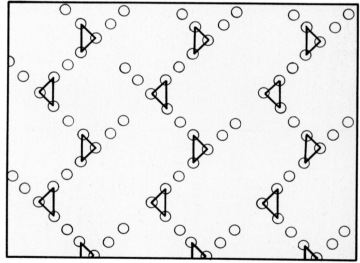

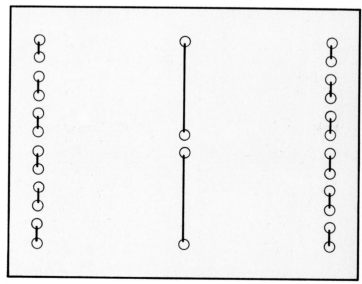

*Ribbon weaving patterns: top, style 1; middle, style 2; and bottom, style 3.*

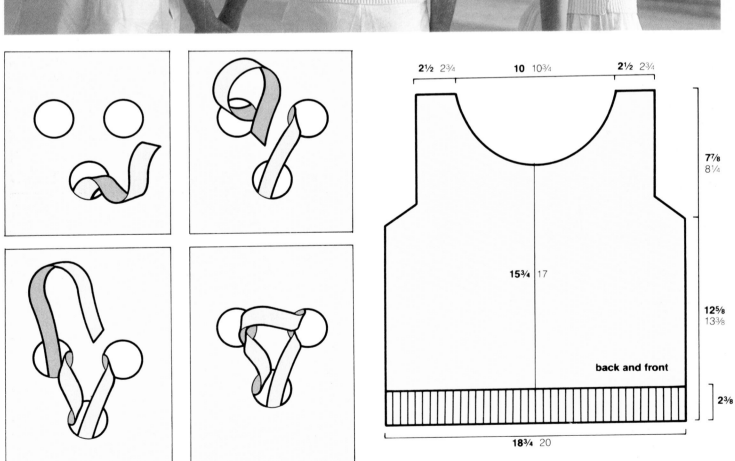

2½  2¾   **10**  10¾   2½  2¾

**7⅞**
8¼

**15¾** 17

**12⅝**
13⅜

**back and front**

**2⅜**

**18¾** 20

# PAINTBOX CARDIGAN

A glorious palette of subtly matched colors. You can achieve the sophisticated gradation of shades without vast expense by using small skeins of tapestry wools for the squares. Fronts and sleeves are patterned all over with the little boxes, while the back has a simpler arrangement of just seven. For the perfect finishing touch, find buttons in various colors to match the samples in the nearby rows.

## CHECKLIST

### Materials

*Berger du Nord 4-ply: 10 (11) balls ecru (**E**) (if this yarn is unobtainable refer to pages 78-9).*
*Laine Colbert DMC: one 8 m (9 yd) skein in each of the foll colors:*
*7102 7103 7104 7106 7107 7132 7136 7137 7138 7139 7151 7153 7155 7157 7194 7204 7205 7212 7241 7243 7245 7247 7253 7255 7257 7259 7296 7340 7341 7342 7344 7361 7362 7363 7369 7370 7371 7386 7399 7423 7425 7431 7433 7435 7436 7437 7493 7512 7540 7544 7548 7549 7595 7596 7597 7598 7600 7602 7604 7606 7666 7678 7679 7680 7681 7740 7741 7791 7797 7798 7800 7807 7860 7861 7905 7909 7912 7943 7946 7971 7973 7988*
*For the larger size you will also need a skein each of 7314, 7316, 7318, 7820. Pair each of needles size 2 and 4; 6 buttons.*
*Note on colors You can if you prefer use fewer colors; each square only needs approx 4 yards – 3.5 meters and each skein is sufficient for 2 squares. You can work out a different arrangement of colors using our charts as a guide.*

### Sizes

*Two sizes, to fit bust 32/34 (36/38) in; 82/87 (92/97) cm. Actual measurements shown on diagram.*

### Stitches used

*Single rib; st st. For each square wind off 4 yards of the correct color; wind this onto a piece of cardboard, cut a slit in the card and pass the end through to prevent it becoming tangled. Also use a small ball of **E** for the sections between the squares. Join on the balls as required and always twist the yarns around each other when changing color. On completion of a square cut off any spare yarn leaving an end for darning in later.*

### Tension

*Over st st using size 4 needles and either yarn, 23 sts and 30 rows to 4 in (10 cm). Work a sample on 28 sts.*

## INSTRUCTIONS

### BACK

▦ With size 2 needles and **E** cast on 115 (123) sts and work in rib.
▦ *1st row* (right side). P 1, * k 1, p 1; rep from * to end.
▦ *2nd row* K 1, * p 1, k 1; rep from * to end. Rep these 2 rows until work measures 1¼ in (3 cm) from beg, ending with a 2nd rib row but inc 1 st in center of last row. 116 (124) sts. Change to size 4 needles and beg with a k row work in st st until 48 (54) rows have been worked then begin 1st square at center.
▦ *1st row* K 52 (56) **E**, join on color for 1st square as shown on chart, k 12 with this color, join on

another ball of **E**, k 52 (56) **E**. Cont as set for 14 more rows then cut off remainder of the color and using one ball of **E** only work 9 rows in st st.
▦ *25th row* K 36 (39) **E**, join on color for next square and k 12 with this, join on another ball of **E** and k 20 (22), join on color for next square, k 12 with this, join on another ball of **E**, k 36 (39) **E**. Cont with these 2 squares for 14 more rows then work 9 rows in **E**.
▦ *49th row* K 20 (22) **E**, join on color for next square, k 12 with this, k 52 (56) **E**, join on color for next square, k 12 with this, join on another ball of **E**, k 20 (22) **E**. Cont with these 2 squares for 14 more rows then work 9 rows in **E**.
▦ *73rd row* K 4 (5) **E**, join on color for next square and k 12 with this, k 84 (90) **E**, join on color for next square and k 12 with this, join on another ball of **E**, k 4 (5) **E**. Cont as now set for 5 more rows; 126 (132) rows have been worked in st st.
▦ **Armhole Shaping** Cast off 4 sts at beg of next 2 rows and 2 sts at beg of next 4 rows. 100 (108) sts.

Work 3 more rows with the sts rem from each square in correct color, then using **E** only work 49 (51) rows in **E**; 184 (192) rows have been worked in st st.
▦ **Neck and Shoulder Shaping**
*1st row* K 42 (45) and leave these sts of right back on needle, cast off next 16 (18) sts, k to end. Cont on 42 (45) sts now rem at end of needle for left back and work 1 row straight. ** Cast off 6 sts at beg of next row.
▦ Now for shoulder cast off 11 sts at beg of next row and 2 sts at neck edge on foll row; rep last 2 rows once. Cast off rem 10 (13) sts to complete shoulder slope. Rejoin yarn to neck edge of right back sts and complete as for left back from ** to end.

### LEFT FRONT

▦ With size 2 needles and **E** cast on 61 (65) sts and work in rib as on back welt for same number of rows and inc 1 st in center of last row. 62 (66) sts. Change to size 4 needles and working in st st begin 1st line of squares in the 3 colors

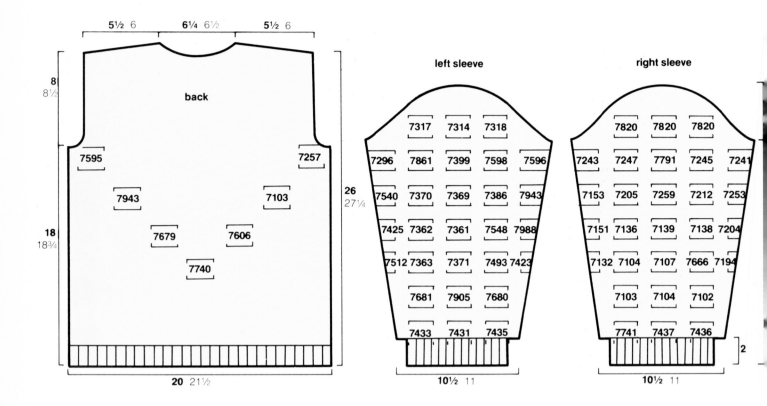

indicated, joining on these colors and small balls of **E** as folls:
▦ *1st row* K 7 (8) **E**, work 1st square, k 6 (7) **E**, work 2nd square, k 6 (7) **E**, work 3rd square, k 7 (8) **E**. Work 14 more rows as now set then work 9 rows in **E**. Cont working the lines of squares in the colors shown on chart always placing them above each other and with 9 rows in **E** between each completed line of squares and the next. Cont until 122 (128) rows have been worked in st st thus ending with a p row.
▦ **Front and Armhole Shaping**
*1st row* K to last 4 sts, SKPO, k 2. Cont to dec in this position on every foll 4th row 3 (4) times. *At same time*, keep side edge straight until 126 (132) rows have been worked then cast off 4 sts at beg of next row and 2 sts at same edge on next 2 alt rows. When the 4 (5) decs at front have been worked, cont to dec at the actual front edge on next 8 alt rows then on every foll 3rd row 10 times. Cont on rem 32 (35) sts until 186 (194) rows have been worked in st st; for the 1st size 3 rows in **E** have

been worked after completing 8th line of squares and for the 2nd size 2 rows of the 9th line of squares have been worked.
▦ **Shoulder Shaping** For 1st size cont with **E** only; for 2nd size cont in patt. Cast off 11 sts at beg of next row and next alt row, work 1 row then cast off rem 10 (13) sts.

**RIGHT FRONT**
▦ Work as for left front arranging squares in same way but using colors as shown on right front chart. Begin front shaping on same row as for left front and for the first 4 (5) decs work k 2, k 2 tog, k to end, working rem decs at actual front edge as on left front. Begin armhole and shoulder shaping 1 row after those of left front.

**RIGHT SLEEVE**
▦ With size 2 needles and **E** cast on 49 (53) sts and work in rib as on back but cont until work measures 2 in (5 cm) from beg, ending with a 1st rib row.
▦ *Inc row* Rib 4 (6), [inc in next st, rib 3] 10 times, inc in next st, rib 4

(6). 60 (64) sts. Change to size 4 needles and working in st st begin 1st line of squares in the 3 colors indicated.
▦ *1st row* K 6 (7) **E**, k 12 in 1st color, k 6 (7) **E**, k 12 in 2nd color, k 6 (7) **E**, k 12 in 3rd color, k 6 (7) **E**. Cont as now set but inc 1 st at both ends of every foll 10th row 1 (4) times, then every foll 8th row 13 (10) times. Work lines of squares as shown on chart always with 9 rows in **E** between them, beg new squares at sides on 49th row. When incs are completed cont on 88 (92) sts until 122 (128) rows have been worked in st st.
▦ **Top Shaping** Cast off 4 sts at beg of next 2 rows and 2 sts at beg of next 32 (34) rows. Cast off rem 16 sts.

**LEFT SLEEVE**
▦ Work as for right sleeve but using the colors shown in chart for left sleeve.

**FRONT AND NECK BORDERS**
▦ With right side facing and using size 2 needles and **E**, pick up and k 113 (118) sts along straight front

edge of right front and 66 (69) sts along sloping edge to shoulder. Beg with 2nd row work in rib as on back welt and after working 3 rows make buttonholes.
▦ *Next row* Beg at lower edge, right side facing, rib 6, cast off 3, [rib until there are 17 (18) sts on right needle after previous buttonhole, cast off 3] 5 times, rib to end. On foll row cast on 3 sts over each buttonhole. Work 3 more rows in rib then cast off loosely ribwise. Work similar border on left front picking up sts in reverse order and omitting buttonholes. With right side facing, using size 2 needles and **E**, pick up and k 41 (43) sts across back neck. Beg with 2nd row work 8 rows in rib then cast off loosely ribwise.

**MAKING UP**
▦ Join shoulder seams and ends of borders. Sew in sleeves then join side and sleeve seams. Sew on buttons to correspond with buttonholes.

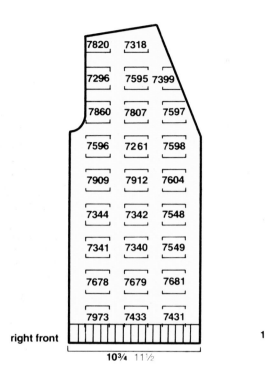

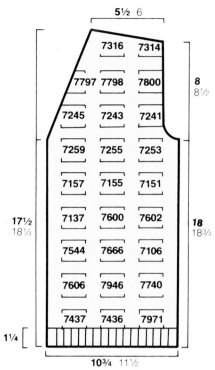

right front

*If you feel that you cannot afford the luxury of using such a wide range of colors, make several copies of these diagrams and color them in with a more limited range of shades, keeping to the basic arrangement of blocks of reds, blues, greens and yellows.*

# YARN OPTIONS

The yarns used to knit some of the designs in this book may be difficult to obtain outside France. If you have problems in finding the listed yarns, the substitutes given below would be perfectly acceptable alternatives. Colors change with the seasons, so do not be worried if you cannot use exactly the same shades as the original: the designer was equally limited by what was available at the first time of making, and there is no reason why the pattern should not look even prettier in the colors of your own choosing. After all, you are the best person to judge what suits you.

*Ming Jersey*

## MING JERSEY

*3 Suisses Shirley: 7 (8) balls shade 61, black (**B**) and 5 (6) balls shade 14 blue (**A**). Pair each of needles size 1 and 2.*

## WOVEN ROSES

*3 Suisses Shirley: 9 balls beige No 58 (**A**) and 8 balls yellow No 36 (**B**). For the flowers: Carina Yves St Laurent: 1 ball red No 76 and 1 ball dark wine No 02. Pair each of needles size 1 and 2.*

## WISTERIA CARDIGAN

*Pingouin Pingofrance: 9 (10) balls Nuage No 113 (**A**), 3 balls Lilas (mauve) No 218 (**B**), 1 ball Jade No 106 (**C**). Pair each of needles size 1, 2 and 3; 4 buttons; pair of shoulder pads.*

## ETHNIC AFRICA

*Pingouin Pingofrance: for style 1 with yellow as main color, 9 balls jonquille No 174 (**Y**), and 4 balls noir No 133 (**B**). For style 2 with black as main color, 8 balls noir No 133 (**B**), and 5 balls jonquille No 174 (**Y**). Pair each of needles size 2 and 3.*

## CINEMASCOPE JERSEY

*Pingouin Pingolaine: 10(11) balls noir No 15, black, and 1 ball brun No 69, brown. For the remaining colours only small amounts are needed; in each case we give the shade number and also name the colour so that you can locate it more easily on the charts. Small amounts only of Vert Deau No 06 pale green; Giroselle No 19, yellow Lagon No 50, deep blue; Glacier No 05, pale blue; Nuage No 62, pale grey; orange No 64; Citron No 58, yellow; beige rose No 34, pale tan; azàlee No 65, dark pink; eglantine No 54, salmon pink. Pair each of needles size 2¼mm and 3mm.*

## TECHNICOLOR MOHAIR

MULTICOLORED COAT
*Pingouin Confort: 10 (11) balls noir No 156 (**A**); Pingouin Mohair 50: 9 (10) balls noir No 532 (**B**); Pingouin Pingofrance: 1 ball in each of the foll. feu No 131 (**C**), red; azalée No 217 (**D**), fuchsia pink; cobalt No 127 (**E**), bright blue; flamme No 216 (**F**), orange; changai No 201 (**G**), violet; vert vif No 176 (**H**), bright green, and jonquille No 174 (**J**), yellow. Pair each of needles size 5 and 7; a cable needle; 2 buttons.*

## ROLL COLLAR DRESS

*Pingouin Orage: 17 (18) balls feu No 109. Pair each of needles size 5 and 7.*

*Woven Roses*

*Wisteria Cardigan*

*Ethnic Africa*

*Cinemascope Jersey*

## JAPANESE WAVE

*Pingouin* Confort: *5 balls amiral No 107* (**1**)*, blue black; 3 balls ecru No 131* (**7**)*; 2 balls nuage No 173* (**4**)*, silver gray; 2 balls grège No 117* (**3**)*, mid gray; 2 balls souris No 135* (**2**)*, mouse; 1 ball or part ball dragée No 175* (**5**)*, pale pink; azur No 163* (**11**)*, light blue; glacier No 106* (**12**)*, pale blue; and cyprès No 120* (**10**)*, blue green.* Pingouin *Pingofrance: ball or part ball giroselle No 19* (**6**)*, brown; givre No 212* (**13**)*, onyx; bleu franc 128* (**9**)*, bright blue, and cobalt No 127* (**8**)*, deep blue. Pair each of needles size 2 and 4.*

## THIRTIES FAVOURITES
## THE WAFFLE

*Pingouin* Fil d'Ecosse No 3: *10 (11-11) balls. Pair each of needles size 2 and 6.*

## AT THE RUSSIAN BALLET

*Pingouin* Pingofine: *8 balls noir No 333* (**A**)*; 3 balls jade No 306* (**B**)*; 3 balls feu No 331* (**C**)*, red; 2 balls azur No 326* (**D**)*, blue; 3 balls vieux rose No 339* (**E**)*, rose; and 1 ball poussin No 335* (**F**)*, straw.* Pingouin *Luciole: 11 balls Or No 01* (**G**)*, gold. To replace the color champagne use 1 strand of* Pingofine *vieux rose and 1 strand of* Luciole *shade Or together, this is referred to as* **H***. Pair each of needles size 5 and 6.*

## SHE SELLS SCALLOP SHELLS
## SCALLOP SHELL SWEATER

*Pingouin* Coton Naturel 8 fils: *16 balls in ecru* (**E**) *and 4 balls in white* (**W**)*.* Pingouin *Coton Naturel 4 fils: 3 balls in white. This is used for shells. Pair each of needles size 3, 4 and 6; a cable needle.*

## SHELL MOTIF SWEATER

*Pingouin* Corrida 4: *15 (16) balls bonbon No 504. Pair each of needles size 3 and 4; a circular needle size 4 in order to accommodate all sts for the full width of sweater.*

## GIANT JUMPER

*Pingouin* Pingostar: *25 balls in desired color; pair of needles size 9; set of double-pointed needles in same size for neck border.*

## PAINTBOX CARDIGAN

*Pingouin* Pingofrance: *9 (10) balls ecru No 153* (**E**)*.* Laine Colbert DMC *as listed on page 74.*

*At The Russian Ballet*

*Japanese Wave*

*The Waffle*

*Scallop Shell Sweater*

*Shell Motif Sweater*

*Technicolor Mohair*

*Roll Collar Dress*

*Giant Jumper*

*Paintbox Cardigan*

# STOCKISTS

If you have difficulty obtaining the specified yarns in your area, the agents and stockists listed below may be able to help you either by supplying the yarn directly to you or by giving you the name of your local supplier.

**BERGER DU NORD**
Brookman & Sons Inc, 4416 North East 11th Avenue, Fort Lauderdale, Florida 33334

**GEORGES PICAUD USA**
Merino Wool Co. Inc., 230 Fifth Avenue, Suite 2000, New York, NY 10001 Tel. 212-686-0050

**LAINES ANNY BLATT INC.**
24770 Crestview Court, Farmington Hills, Michigan 48018 Tel. 313-474-2942

**LES FILATURES DE PARIS**
Zamart, 11 West 37th Street, New York, NY 10001

**PINGOUIN**
Promofil Corp (USA), 9179 Red Branch Road, Columbia, Maryland 21045 Tel. 301-730-0101

**3 SUISSE**
Dominique Corp., Empire State Building, Suite 2709, 350 Fifth Avenue, New York, NY 10018